HOWARD RODWAY

The Psychic Directory

Futura
Macdonald & Co
London & Sydney

A Futura Book

First published in Great Britain in 1984 by
Futura Publications, a Division of
Macdonald & Co (Publishers) Ltd
London & Sydney

ISBN 0 7088 2454 4

Filmset, printed and bound in Great Britain by
Hazell Watson & Viney Limited,
Member of the BPCC Group,
Aylesbury, Bucks

Futura Publications
A Division of
Macdonald & Co (Publishers) Ltd
Maxwell House
74 Worship Street
London EC2A 2EN
A BPCC plc Company

Born in Surrey in 1936, Howard Rodway has had a varied life, spending many months travelling before settling down in the Foreign Office for several years. His interest in psychic experiences really began when he met the late Joseph Benjamin, whose astonishing claim that Mr Rodway had a sister was discovered years later to be true. He has worked with the renowned clairvoyant Kim Tracey, and his own psychic experiences have been related in *Psychic News*.

Mr Rodway lives in Kent with his wife Marie Térèse.

For
Joseph Benjamin
and
two ex-cypher operators: BP and DK

Sadly, medium Joseph Benjamin passed away in
mid 1983. The loss of this dynamic medium will
be felt for years to come. For many the void will
be permanent. Joseph Benjamin set an example
of mediumship at its very best and changed
countless lives for the better.
Thank you, Joe.

CONTENTS

ACKNOWLEDGEMENTS

Macdonald & Co Publishers, for making this project possible; medium, the late Joseph Benjamin who gave encouragement and advice when this Directory was at the embryo stage; Daniel J. Cronin for the loan of books from his private collection of psychic and psychic-related literature; *Psychic News* Editor Tony Ortzen for his interest and for his contributions; Ron Laing, M.A., for his *Note on Satya Sai Baba*, Sai Ram Centre Manager R. Kapur for his contributions to the Sai Baba chapter; Samantha, who spent long hours composing answers to questions on such subjects as reincarnation, spirit guides and healing; The Spiritualists' National Union General Secretary Charles S. Coulston and *The Greater World Christian Spiritualist Weekly* Editor Annette Clifton, for contributions including their respective church philosophies and principles, together with church listings; The Minority Rights Group, for permission to quote a section from their *Report No. 31: The Original Americans: US Indians* by James Wilson; Marie Térèse for typing services rendered above and beyond the call of duty.

Heartfelt thanks must obviously also be extended to all the mediums, psychics, healers and astrologers who have made this book the Directory that it is.

THIS IS THEIR DIRECTORY.

INTRODUCTION

Over the years, I have been asked all manner of questions about the psychic world. Some of those enquirers wanted to find clairvoyants or healers, others wanted to be put in touch with their nearest Spiritualist church or centre, and some wanted to find books dealing with specific areas of psychic activity.

Spurred on by these constant and continuing queries, the idea grew in my mind that I could provide an information service for enquirers and psychics alike. The most readily available information had to be in book form, so the project evolved into *The Psychic Directory*. The deeper value of this book will hopefully be to provide a starting point and a route for those seeking a direction, for the psychic world provides possibilities for the journey of a lifetime.

In this Directory you will find diviners and healers listed together with traditional Spiritualist mediums. You will also find astrologers, some of whom are psychic astrologers and some who are astrologer-psychics. There are also mediums who use what are technically non-Spiritualist methods of divination. This may upset a few purists, but in my experience, there will be less criticism from those who are secure in their own field of activity, than from those who are not. The important point is that all should be sincerely motivated to help others. One of the joys of compiling this book has been to witness the response from psychics of various backgrounds. My other great satisfaction has been the response from diviners of the Moslem, Hindu and Jewish faiths etc. All are to be found under one 'roof'.

I make no excuses if all this sounds a little idealistic, for this book is the end product of an ideal: which is to help others as I was once helped when a new (but very old) dimension was revealed.

Spiritualist churches, centres and associations are also listed here, together with publications and bookshops that deal with psychic and psychic-related subjects. There is a chapter about *Psychic News* with an introduction by its editor, Tony Ortzen. This particular chapter also contains a slightly abridged version of an article that appeared in *Psychic News*, highlighting past royal family connections with Spiritualism. Special mention is made of Eastern mystic and holy man Sai Baba, while other chapters deal with psychic experiences, reincarnation, spirit guides, healing and the spiritual philosophy of the North American Indian.

Kind thoughts and a safe journey,

Howard Rodway

I

Psychic Experiences

I had little or no time for psychic activities until the early '60s and even then I started by being a less than enthusiastic observer at a public demonstration of clairvoyance. The demonstrating medium was the late Joseph Benjamin. The name meant nothing to me then, but this gifted medium was soon to have a very influential effect on my life.

The sequence of events started when I made some silly remarks to an office acquaintance of mine who was trying to make intelligent conversation on the subject of Spiritualism. We were both Foreign Office cypher operators at the time. On this particular occasion we were sharing the tedium of a Sunday duty. In response to my inane remarks, he invited me along to a public demonstration of clairvoyance – to judge for myself. He also volunteered to pay the modest admission charge for both of us. I had little choice but to accept his invitation unless I wanted to lose face, so the following Sunday evening was put aside to see Joseph Benjamin demonstrate clairvoyance.

A day or so later I discussed the subject with another cypher operator, a lively personality who brought a refreshing element of her native West Country to our uninspiring little Whitehall office. She was later to witness a demonstration of clairvoyance by the same medium that we were about to see. Little did we know at the time that our own section chief was psychic and must have been quietly amused at our sudden interest in 'other world' activities.

The outcome of seeing Joseph Benjamin demonstrate clairvoyance was that I booked to see him privately. His abilities had impressed me, and my office chum suggested that a private consultation would provide the 'conclusive proof' to show that what I had witnessed was genuine.

My first private consultation with Joseph Benjamin provided enough proof to make me realize that the psychic world had a far deeper significance than the average person, myself included, was aware of.

Joseph Benjamin started the sitting by telling me that my great grandfather was present, while at the same time adding a perfect description of the old gentleman. After accurately tracing my childhood and early adulthood, he moved on to the circumstances that surrounded me at the time. The latter part of the sitting concerned future events, and during his projection into my future, he suddenly interrupted himself to say, 'You have a sister.'

At the end of the sitting I disputed this piece of information, pointing out that I was an only child. Joseph Benjamin just looked at me and said, 'Check the records at Somerset House and you will find that what I say is correct – you have a sister.'

I doubt whether it would have been possible to check the records at that time for such information was highly confidential, so I let the matter slip for several years until I eventually asked my mother. She gave a firm denial and was obviously not amused that I could even consider taking a clairvoyant seriously! Her anger inhibited any further discussion, and so the subject rested until 1977.

The years went by and my interest in the psychic had developed to the point where I was receiving my own psychic impressions.

Through this interest, I got to know Medway-based clairvoyant Kim Tracey. During the latter part of 1977, she told me that I would be in America within six months – and by an odd set of circumstances that prediction came to pass. I wrote to her, telling her that I was making travel arrangements to go to Hollywood and she phoned to say that she would be in Beverly Hills at the same time and suggested that we meet out there.

Contrary to popular belief, Hollywood is not the most enchanting area of Los Angeles, therefore I was very pleased to take the opportunity of visiting Kim in Beverly Hills. We met for lunch and then arranged to see each other again. It was at our final meeting in Beverly Hills that Kim made me a most unusual job offer. She asked me if I would look after public relations for her during an anticipated busy period a few months ahead. She told me to think carefully about the offer and then to let her have a decision after her return to England. I quickly mentioned that I knew nothing about PR work, to which she replied, 'You'll do very well because you can communicate with people and you understand the work that I do.' She added, 'Howard, don't forget that I *am* a clairvoyant – I know that you will do well.' This unusual conversation took place on Sunday morning outside a well-known actor's house in the heart of residential Beverly Hills!

To cut a long story short, I accepted Kim's offer and it turned out to be an extremely interesting period. I arrived on the scene just before the publication of Kim's auto-biography: *Secrets of the Runes*. The pace was frantic, and we were constantly rushing here, there and everywhere. I developed an enormous respect for Kim's hard-working routine, for she never allowed herself a break if there was work to be done or someone to see. The publication of her autobiography meant an even more rigorous period of activity and we must have covered the entire country in hectic promotional tours. It was on one such trip that the strangest drama occurred.

During early April 1979, we were in Scotland for Kim to appear as a guest on *BBC Radio Glasgow*. This trip was combined with a quick journey to her childhood home in Glenglass.

On our homeward journey, we were travelling through the Grampian Mountains when some very unusual inci-dents happened. There were four of us in the car and we all commented on the blizzard which had suddenly started without any warning at all. Stranger still was the fact that not one flake of snow seemed to be touching the car, and the windscreen remained completely clear. Looking out of my side window, I noticed a gigantic illuminated Celtic

5

cross which was out beyond the road. This huge cross gave out a brilliant yellow-white light and the beautiful effect was marred by one imperfection: a vivid red line cut a jagged pattern through the cross-spar. As we motored through the blizzard, two vehicles passed us travelling in the opposite direction. We noticed that they were not leaving any tracks in the snow, yet on checking through our rear window, it was quite noticeable that we were leaving heavy tracks. A mile or two on we noticed a white-on-green road sign which indicated that Perth was 108 miles away. We clocked five miles before passing another white-on-green sign which said that Perth was still 108 miles away! Suddenly the blizzard stopped as abruptly and mysteriously as it had started and we continued travelling through the night in a more relaxed frame of mind.

On the following Monday, a local Medway mechanic examined the Jaguar in which we had been travelling. He disputed the fact that the car had been through a blizzard because he could find no tell-tale signs on the bodywork!

I decided to do a little checking and phoned the *Inverness Courier*. The editor stated that there had been no blizzard in the area on that night and quoted a Met. Office report which recorded that weather conditions had been normal for the time of year. Furthermore, he assured me that there was no large Celtic cross in the area, certainly not of the proportions that I had described.

Kim has always felt that the cross was a sign of protection. I am convinced that we found ourselves in a situation over which we had no control, a situation which was probably 'engineered' in order to keep us clear of some very unpleasant tragedy. Whatever force rode with us that night, that force was a welcome friend!

One night during 1977, I came home late to be told by my wife that I had two visitors. She would not say who they were, so I went into the sitting room to find a man and a woman waiting. The woman spoke first, saying, 'Are you Howard?' I replied that I was, and then she smiled and said, 'I'm your sister.'

Her statement was so direct and unexpected that I must

have been standing there looking like an idiot. I just did not know what to say. My sister was highly amused and her husband Ian was grinning from ear to ear. When I had a chance to collect my wits, the first thing that I noticed was that my sister bore a strong resemblance to my/our mother. It took me some time to realize that I was actually talking to my own sister – and that we had the same mother and father. She told me that she had been adopted as a tiny baby and that she had been brought up with no real idea of her true parental background. She went on to say that she had taken advantage of the change in the adoption law which had then allowed her access to records. Her search for family roots had uncovered the fact that she had a brother, so she eventually found out where I was living. We had a lot to talk about and we chatted until five in the morning. Much of our conversation centred on Joseph Benjamin's prediction.

I phoned Joe to tell him the good news and at a later date we were able to see him at the Alliance Hall in London. We were pleased to be able to give personal testimony to his amazing gifts. A *Psychic News* journalist was present and *PN* was the first publication to print the story.

I have talked a lot about Joseph Benjamin and Kim Tracey because both these gifted people are part of my personal story. Let me now bring the record up-to-date and mention the other mediums, psychics and healers who are listed in this book. Their interest, support and assistance has been instrumental in making this a more exciting project than it would have been without such a response. I also want to mention the astrologers who are listed, for they have shown just as much interest and given just as much encouragement. Some of their clients have shown similar enthusiasm for this project, and they have expressed this by writing to me about some of the readings that they have had. A number of these accounts are retold here and some of their letters are quoted. All make fascinating reading and all reflect the help and comfort that consultants are able to provide.

In the mid '70s, Dr John Best was conducting psychic research into the next life and the spirit world. He was in touch with various mediums who were relaying information to him from his fiancée Marjorie who had been 'killed' in a car crash some years before.

His research involved comparing the information he received from various mediums, while at the same time noting how this information 'fitted in with modern science!' His research project eventually brought him into contact with medium Millicent Young.

During the time that he was in contact with Millicent Young, he discussed his investigative project with a friend and fellow scientist. His colleague was impressed enough to devise a test that would, he suggested, make a decisive judgement on Mrs Young's mediumship. He then produced a fragment of stone which he proposed should be given to Mrs Young for psychometry purposes. The fragment was duly given to Mrs Young after she had agreed to undergo the test.

With the stone at hand, Mrs Young began by describing a large house set in its own grounds – she stated that this residence was near Esher. She added that the house was full of collectors' items. She then turned her psychic attention to a gentleman not known to Dr Best but, so she said, a relation of the doctor's friend. Mrs Young described this person by his physical build and style of dress. She was in fact decribing someone who was no longer physically alive. She next received an impression of a sandy place, high on a rock. She was uncertain of just where this was, except that it was obviously a foreign location. In the distance she could see shapes that reminded her of pyramids but she stated that the area in question was not Egypt. Then she concentrated on the rock, describing things that looked like water tanks. These were set deep inside the rock, and she emphasized her impression of these tanks as though it was of importance. Dr Best was mystified by this information. She finally noted that the stone had been taken from the sandy area on top of the rock. Dr Best had taken copious notes during Mrs Young's reading of the stone, and later informed his friend and fellow scientist that none of the information meant much to him. Nevertheless, he gave his colleague a full account of what Mrs Young had said.

After Dr Best had given a stage by stage run-down on the reading from the stone, his friend was able to confirm that the house that had been mentioned was his childhood home, and that the property was still owned by his family. The relative was without a doubt his father who had been in the RAF and who had travelled widely, bringing home many objects – including the stone! The pyramid-like objects presented him with no problems of identification – they would be the hills of Judaea – because Mrs Young had received the impression of standing on the famous Rock of Masada on which Herod's palace had once stood. She had seen the hills opposite and rain catchment tanks below in the rock – excavated to provide a reservoir for the palace! The scientist's father had picked up the rock fragment from the site upon which the palace had been built!

Dr Best remarks that 'it was a striking experience for me' to have the story confirmed by someone who knew nothing of Millicent Young. He also adds that his friend was, 'very much impressed by my studies'. Dr Best records that he was certainly surprised that Millicent Young was able to analyse the rock, but came to the conclusion that her knowledge came by way of mind-to-mind contact with his friend's father – a man who no longer existed physically.

The original account of this story was kindly sent by:
J. E. Best, Ph.D. (Cantab), B.Sc. (London),
Wallingford Road,
South Stoke.

High Praise from the Lowlands

The following story is from a Hollander, and let me add here that Holland not only seems to produce some very gifted psychics, but generally speaking, the Dutch also seem to be far more open-minded than ourselves on the subject of the psychic. This point was brought home when clairvoyant Kim Tracey first stepped onto Dutch soil and received an intelligent and warm-hearted response from all sections of the community. I am therefore very pleased to quote the following letter which arrived from the Netherlands during the preparation of this book.

On my request Jackie Durnin made in 1980 the chart of my little nephew Arvid (born 1979 in the Netherlands). It is a well-written, clear horoscope with very useful advice regarding his care and education.

From his birth on, Arvid suffered from a serious eczema. He itched, scratched his skin to open, slept uneasily (awoke often five times a night – crying), was very nervous and strained. The physicians could offer less help because the boy was too small for a profound examination.

In the beginning of 1982 I applied to Jackie Durnin once more for a personal problem analysis. Her astrological work and dream interpretation including her attendance are very valuable to me so that I have much confidence in her. Therefore because she also sends absent healing I asked her help for the toddler in May '82.

Jackie Durnin sent absent healing to the child (without a photo and living far away) and practical and helpful advice too.

Now after some time (October '82) Arvid is better, cheerful, relaxed, sleeps well, and as I have actually seen, because I sometimes look after the boy for some days, his eczema has practically disappeared.

Client of Jackie Durnin,
The Netherlands,
October 1982.

A Shining Example

If there is someone who should have an exceptionally bright aura, that someone must be Mrs Barbara Burnard of Pennycross, Plymouth. Over the months, several letters have arrived to endorse her gifts of healing and clairvoyancy. Here are some direct quotes from Plymouth:

> On one occasion I was suffering bad back pains at work, when all of a sudden Mrs Burnard came into the store. She sensed my distress and gave me some healing. Within a matter of hours I felt 100% better. This has happened on several occasions with the same results . . .
> I feel it essential you should list her name amongst your healers so that others may experience the tremendous warmth and comfort that I felt.
>
> Jill Coleman.

Mrs Dawn Szmydt of Penarth, South Wales is also able to tell of the benefit derived from Mrs Burnard's healing power. Mrs Szmydt had been working as a beauty consultant when the opportunity arose to realize a longstanding ambition to become an air stewardess. A few weeks after joining the airline, she became uncomfortably aware of pain around her ears, nose and head. She had no history of sinus trouble and various doctors were unable to help her with the problem. One evening, though, she came into contact with Mrs Burnard who gave her some healing. – Barbara Burnard applied finger pressure to either side of her nose for 'one agonizing minute'. Nothing happened, so Mrs Szmydt went to bed and thought no more about it. When she got up in the morning she blew her nose and some congealed blood was released, and as she says, 'I felt as though a heavy weight had been lifted from my head. It was great – I had no more trouble and enjoyed two more years of flying!'

Healer-counsellor Mrs Irene Horner of Plymouth (see listing), is also full of praise for Barbara Burnard's gifts, and so also is Mrs Anne Thomas of Peverell, Plymouth, who says, 'She just loves helping people to help themselves. Always ready and kind. Please let others know about her, she will help them.'

A Speight of Good Luck

From West Yorkshire there comes the story of the man who sought the counsel of Freddie Speight. He needed Freddie's advice at a time when he was going through an extremely worrying period in his professional life. His organization had become involved in a particularly nasty take-over drama, and it became obvious to him that his presence was no longer required. He was 'subjected to unpleasantness of the worst kind' and found himself in what he later found out to be an 'engineered' situation – a situation which could have brought professional ruin and wrecked his marriage.

He had known Freddie Speight for 41 years but they had not met recently, so he decided to renew contact and ask Freddie for some advice at the same time. After seeing Freddie, the skies started to clear and the danger was soon past. In addition a loyal colleague who had been fired was later awarded a four figure sum by an industrial tribunal for wrongful dismissal. In fact, events seemed to turn out just the way that Freddie Speight had said they would!

Mr Oldham of Millbridge, Liversedge, West Yorkshire, comments on Freddie Speight's healing power. He came into contact (literally) with Freddie on a day when he was suffering from a bad attack of fibrositis. The discomfort increased as the day wore on, and it was only by chance that Mr Oldham told Freddie of the pain that he was in, not knowing that Freddie was a 'spirit healer'.

Freddie Speight located the exact area of the pain with his hand, and Mr Oldham records what happened; 'I had the strangest experience of my life. I felt my whole body glow and tingle, then the pain left my body as though it was being sucked out.' Within half an hour all pain and soreness had vanished.

It was obviously a Speight of good luck for Mr Oldham on that particular day!

Time is Precious

Michael O'Sullivan has a prized possession, a Rolex Oyster Perpetual watch, which had given him 'sterling' service for over thirty years.

In 1981, he had refused a generous cash offer for his Rolex, for he had no intention of parting with the watch, but trouble started soon after his refusal to sell.

Michael O'Sullivan's Rolex suddenly stopped for the first time – and he was unable to start it functioning again. He sent the watch to his local Rolex agent but the dealer sent it back, saying that it was beyond repair. The London agent came to the same conclusion – the watch could not be mended. Unable to bring himself to throw the watch away, Michael O'Sullivan put the Rolex in a cardboard box where it stayed for four months.

During a conversation about watches, Freddie Speight heard Michael O'Sullivan discussing the fate of his Rolex, so he asked for an opportunity to examine the timepiece. Freddie saw the watch the next day, and, taking it in his left hand, he passed his right hand over the face of the watch, then he said, 'This watch is going.' Michael O'Sullivan couldn't believe it but months and months later that watch is still ticking away. Mr O'Sullivan emphasizes the fact that he is a practising Roman Catholic who does not believe in psychic phenomena – but he also wishes it to be known that the story of his Rolex is perfectly true.

Michael O'Sullivan,
25 October, 1982.

From a Town in Germany

Mrs Betty Dabrowa is one of those people you know instinctively is a good person, a soul who will go out of her way to help others, often at inconvenience to herself. She has been psychically gifted since early childhood and her

13

spiritual 'insights' are amazing. She is particularly adept at past life readings, and one such reading that she gave me has a somewhat uncanny parallel with the early part of my present life!

I am pleased to quote from the following letter, particularly as the correspondent, a doctor, has taken the trouble to write from Bonn in West Germany.

I hope I can express my letter in good English, but I think you'll understand it. First, I knew Mrs Dabrowa only by letters (until 1978). Her readings she gave me without knowing anything about me were true in regard of the past and also present and future. She knew that I'd helped people behind the 'Iron Curtain', and she best of all, she saw my second beloved husband in the spiritual world and could describe him exactly. She painted him and many other souls too. After this, my friends (who had also got readings from Betty) and we invited her to write us in Germany. She made contact with our spiritual guides and with our relatives in the spiritual world. A lot of other people came to get readings from her.

She said to some of us – also to me – that we shall soon practise spiritual healing with much success.

Betty found a spring, later on people found water there.

She is good in painting and drawing spirits, and also persons, being alive, she never had seen. I possess a great number of this pictures, and I could recognize all of that spirits and persons. She also knows circumstances of that ones.

Mrs Dabrowa had been twice in Germany with us and it was a good time for our spiritual development. We are now ourselves able to find our spiritual way and we communicate with our spirits, but we are combined in love and friendship with Betty Dabrowa.

I have to mention that she has strong healing power, and she is able to see devas.

I hope you can use my letter.

Yours truly,
L. Hennig

Many letters have arrived to praise the abilities of the

14

consultants who are listed in this Directory, but it just is not possible to publish every letter because of the limited space available, therefore it is no reflection on those consultants who do not have some letter or account recorded here to praise their gifts. I should point out that, generally speaking, clients are extremely reluctant to discuss the details of private readings. The majority of those who see consultants do so in order to seek help and advice for very personal and intimate problems, so they are unlikely to be willing to 'tell all' to the public. Under the circumstances, I am very grateful to those who have written to me with their accounts and stories – I thank them.

A View from Rochester Bridge

The 7.45 a.m. Gillingham–Victoria train is definitely not my favourite time to travel nor is it my favourite conveyance! The sight of hundreds of depressed faces belonging to reluctant commuters only adds to my own mood of melancholia, but from time to time we all go through phases of self-inflicted purgatory!

When it is necessary for me to travel during the rush hour, I choose to find a quiet space in the train corridor, rather than sit in a crowded compartment.

On and off over the last few years, I must have been looking at the same view from a train corridor window, a view from Rochester Bridge as the train pulls away from the Medway towns for London. On the one side of the bridge is Rochester Harbour, dominated by a chalk cliff with a church perched at the top. This church is quite visible as it stands silhouetted against the skyline. I had gazed at this scene on many occasions and yet I had never really focused my mind on the significance of what I was viewing.

In 1974 I had a dream in which I had to reach the top of a cliff by way of a narrow footpath which ran from the bottom to the top. I started the ascent but I was very apprehensive about losing my balance or slipping over the cliff edge. I succeeded in reaching the cliff top without mishap and there the dream ended.

Normally, one would attribute anxiety or stress as a reason for having such a dream, that is, under 'ordinary' circumstances. In this particular case, though, the dream was to prove to be precognitive, for the cliff and footpath exactly matched the cliff and footpath over which the church stood at the side of Rochester Harbour.

I had my dream in London, long before I had ever visited the Medway area, so the dream held no significance for me at that time. Now it was a different matter!

One Saturday morning I set off to visit the area and I decided that I would take the same route to the cliff top that I had taken in my dream. I started up that footpath with more than a little apprehension and a slight feeling of vertigo, but I reached the top without anything untoward happening. I turned to the left and soon found myself in the church graveyard. I knew what my psychic 'instinct' was telling me to look for, and it wasn't long before I found it.

Wandering among the burial places, I came upon a rather forlorn-looking grave which was adorned with a flat stone and an upright cross – bearing the characteristic circle of a Celtic Cross!

I could find no name inscribed in memory of the person who had been laid to rest. probably many years ago, for the cross had corroded witn age. The only engraving that I could find, visible when the grass was flattened near the stone, was: 'THY WILL BE DONE'.

I took some photographs of the cross which I sent to Samantha, who has made a contribution in a later chapter of this book. This is her account of what happened when the photos were in her possession.

'As I looked at the photographs you enclosed, I got a very strong reaction of ENERGY flow into my hands.' Samantha goes on to explain that she held a close-up shot of the Celtic cross headstone and that the image generated an intense heat which curled the photo within 'three to four seconds', whereas the other photo, which was a distant

16

shot of the Celtic cross, 'needed seven to eight seconds to produce the same curl'.

It is very difficult to come to a conclusion about this latest Celtic cross phenomenon, but of one thing I am sure, this will not be my last close encounter with crosses of the Celtic kind.

2

Psychic News

'None can cheat death as a physical process. Individuals sometimes out of vanity will try to prolong their lives by expensive medical treatment, but using the yardstick of infinity, it is of no avail.' So says journalist Tony Ortzen, editor of the Spiritualist weekly, *Psychic News*, and of its sister monthly magazine, *Two Worlds*. *Psychic News*, which was founded in 1932, now has readers in over fifty countries throughout the world. Basically it covers such areas as Spiritualism, spirit healing, survival after death, telepathy, metal bending and other psychic phenomena. In short, the paper covers the entire paranormal.

Ever since man became a reasoning being, he has tried to foretell the future. In various ancient cultures soothsayers used to consult oracles, the best known of these was the one at Delphi in Greece. Priests and priestesses tried to foretell the future. The Bible also contains references concerning attempts to discover what the future holds. Even today in what the western world considers to be uncivilized societies, witch-doctors are still constantly consulted. The last few years have seen an explosion of interest not only in Spiritualism and the paranormal but also the occult generally. Indeed it is probably true that astrologers, palmists, tea-leaf readers, Tarot card practitioners and others will 'read' bits of the body or use other means which attempt to see what life has in store.

Some would argue it is not possible to foretell the future, and I partly agree. Yet the future *can* sometimes be foreseen, for various individuals are able to escape time as we know it and peek around the corner. Coming events may well cast their shadows, but the future cannot be foreseen with any great accuracy. Man has been granted the God-given gift of free will; he can alter the detail, but not the overall tapestry. There is one factor which is common to all, be they rich or poor, young or old, bad or good. This is an aspect of the future which can be predicted with utter certainty. It is that death awaits all. All men are not equal in life, but in this respect they are. None can cheat death as a physical process. Vain individuals will try to prolong their lives by expensive private medical treatment, but using the yardstick of infinity, all their efforts are to no avail. All will one day breathe their last physical breath. So what awaits? Are men, women and children really snuffed out as quickly as a candle on their deathbed? Is earthly life the sum total of existence? Or can we expect a more glorious, spiritually based existence in a different sphere?

Having investigated Spiritualism and the paranormal for over a decade as a journalist and individual, I am convinced that life on earth is but a grain of sand on the sea-shore when compared to infinity. And that infinity applies to humans. Since the advent of modern Spiritualism in 1848, mediums and the spirit world have both provided evidence that humans survive the grave. The dead have literally materialized in seance rooms. They have brought apports – spirit gifts – and provided physical evidence in a number of ways. For example, the dead have written using a variety of means, including automatic writing and script on slates, etc. The dead have been heard to speak independently of the living at seances. The literature of both psychical research and Spiritualism can leave no doubt to any intelligent, reasoning, fair-minded individual that death is not the end of human life. Today the majority of mediums demonstrate mental phenomena. That is, they 'see,' 'hear' or 'sense' the so-called dead. In reality, freed from physical shackles the dead are so much more alive than we are.

Another important aspect of Spiritualism is the work performed by spirit healers. Today they are allowed to treat the sick and suffering in hospital. Furthermore doctors, provided they adhere to certain provisions, can even refer patients to such practitioners. Again there can be no doubt that spirit healers, aided by those in the spirit world, can effect cures which are seemingly miraculous. In a law-governed universe there can be no miracles. Cures are achieved because harmony is restored to the physical body. Sadly, today many people refuse to accept or realize they are spiritual beings encased in a physical body. They operate on a physical level because they are motivated so to do by the spirit. At death, the spirit merely leaves its earthly frame and moves to higher realms. Incidentally, there is also evidence that animals, particularly domestic creatures, continue to live on a spirit level. Death is no foe. In reality it comes to many as a friend, an angel of mercy who will put an end to all physical suffering.

In a carefully regulated universe it would be a shame if humankind did not survive the grave. Nature, with all its intricacies, is a marvel of creation. The seasons come and go. The sun and moon rise and fall. The tides go in and out. Day manifests, to be replaced by night. The stars continue to shine at night. On all levels, life operates within the most marvellously created laws. Could it really be that man is not included in them? That in such a superbly created and run environment, he will live his three score years and ten, and then die, to live no further? Even on this level I must accept that man, an integral part of the universe, will survive. Survival after death is at the heart of major religions. Spiritualism differs in that it claims to offer evidence of immortality. Throughout the world, mediums regularly demonstrate that those joined by love truly can never be separated by death.

Tony Ortzen,
Editor, *Psychic News*.

Right Royal Psychic Stories for Prince Charles to Tell his Son

Pam Riva

When ex-Prime Minister Benjamin Disraeli lay dying, every day he received flowers and messages from Queen Victoria.

Towards his earthly end, the monarch asked if she might visit her beloved 'Dizzy'.

Turning his face to the wall, Disraeli murmured, 'No, it is better not. She will only want me to take a message to Albert.'

This extravagance reveals a side of Britain's great monarch that is unknown to many. For Victoria, Queen of Great Britain and Ireland, Empress of India and Defender of the Faith, was a convinced Spiritualist. In fact, she attended seances two years before modern Spiritualism's birth in 1848!

Evidence of this lies in the gold watch she had engraved for an otherwise unknown psychic. Its inscription runs: 'Presented by Her Majesty to Miss Georgiana Eagle for her meritorious and extraordinary clairvoyance produced at Osborne House, Isle of Wight, July 13th, 1846.'

Miss Eagle passed on before the watch could be presented to her. The Queen's experiences with other mediums convinced her spirit communication was possible.

Assumed names given

In 1861 Queen Victoria had need for her Survival conviction. She was devastated when Prince Albert, her beloved consort, passed.

Soon she learned that messages purporting to come from him had been received at a home circle, for one sitter printed the story in the newspaper he edited.

The medium was R. J. Lees, then still in his teens.

The Queen sent two court officials to the young man's home. They asked for a sitting, giving assumed names.

Lees was not long in trance before he was controlled by an entity who greeted the two courtiers as his friends, using their correct names. He gave the highest Masonic handshake, which young Lees did not know.

The spirit visitor correctly said the courtiers came from the Queen. At first they denied it, but the pair were given such conclusive evidence the control was Prince Albert they admitted the monarch had sent them.

When the courtiers returned to Windsor, the Queen too was convinced for some details the spirit visitor relayed were known only to Albert and herself. The monarch was also impressed by a letter written later through Lees' hand. It was signed with a name used only by Albert to his wife.

The Queen sent for Lees. Albert quickly controlled the young medium and spoke through his lips. According to respected Spiritualist historian Arthur Findlay, Victoria told her husband she wished Lees to remain permanently at Court so he would be available as a channel of communication at all times. The Prince objected. Albert did not wish Lees to be his medium. He could speak to his wife just as well through the son of one of her Scottish ghillies, he insisted.

Victoria sent for the young man, whose name was John Brown.

So began one of the most misunderstood friendships of all time. It lasted for thirty-four years.

When John Brown passed, Victoria's inscription over his grave called him 'God's own gift'. She had a statue of him erected at Balmoral Castle which was removed to the churchyard after her death. The Queen kept a record of all that occurred at her sittings with Brown.

Diaries destroyed

Victoria wrote a monograph, hoping for publication. But the Dean of Windsor threatened to resign as Court Chaplain if the monograph was printed. Her Private Secretary, Sir Henry Ponsonby, also objected. He destroyed Brown's diaries to ensure their contents could never become known. But his precautions were incomplete. Journalist Hannen Swaffer was told by Lionel Logue, the speech specialist who cured George VI's stammer and became the King's close friend, that one diary had been missed.

King George discovered it and told Logue he had read it several times, finding it 'very, very interesting'.

Occasionally Victoria sent for R. J. Lees by a courier as she knew both Court and Church were prejudiced against Spiritualism.

The Queen ignored the advice of the Dean of Windsor – Dr Randall Davidson, later to become Archbishop of Canterbury – to discontinue her communications with Prince Albert and brought up her large family to believe in Spiritualism's principles.

Gifts refused

Six copies of Lees' remarkable book, *Through the Mists*, were specially bound at the Queen's request for her to distribute to members of her family. Victoria offered Lees honours, gifts and a comfortable annuity for his lifetime. He refused them all. Shortly before her passing, Her Majesty sent for the medium to thank him for all he had done. On at least five occasions, said Lees' daughter, Prince Albert spoke through her father in his wife's presence.

Has Victoria communicated since her passing?

Her daughter Princess Louise was convinced by many communications received through direct voice medium Leslie Flint.

One sitter retained his anonymity – until his identity was disclosed by a spirit communicator. Announcing herself as Lady Camperdown, she addressed the recipient as James. The man revealed he was John James who, in his youth, had worked as footman to Lady Camperdown. His next post was as house steward to Princess Louise at Kensington Palace. James became one of Leslie Flint's regular sitters. Victoria once thanked him for giving healing to her daughter. A natural healer, he many times relieved Princess Louise's arthritic pain.

The princess asked for a meeting to be arranged with Leslie. For more than an hour they chatted about his work and the evidential messages the princess received from her husband and her royal mother.

Another of Leslie Flint's communicators was John Brown. A tape was made of the ghillie's broad Scots accent as he said, 'When I had associations with this cult I can say I never broke my trust. Lots of people disliked me intensely. Some thought I took great liberties and wrote things trying to give false impressions. Her Majesty was always kind and good and had great respect for me. People in high places tried to suppress things . . . but it's not for me to talk about that now.'

He added, 'We were very close in this work. She had to keep it dark.'

American physical medium Frank Decker's circle also received communications from Queen Victoria.

When a very experienced British Spiritualist, C. K. Shaw, attended, he heard three unconnected sitters describe someone who 'wanted to say something to the Englishman'.

One described a woman over whose head she saw a large V.

Ten minutes later another attendant mentioned a communicator giving the name Victoria. Mr Shaw responded that he knew no one with this name.

Then a third circle member, a woman with a strong German-American accent, became entranced.

Quickly the heavy accent merged into the refined accents of an Englishman, wrote Mr Shaw.

The spirit visitor told him, 'In spite of such active

opposition from my ministers . . . had for many years made a practice of consulting the spirit world on matters of vital importance . . . urge you to continue untiringly and wholeheartedly in your efforts to spread the truth.'

Mr Shaw wrote later, 'All this seemed from a different world. It was without doubt Queen Victoria who was speaking, with her own, independent voice.'

Another medium through whom the ruler spoke in direct voice was Etta Wriedt.

Evidence is engraved on the watch destined for Georgiana Eagle, which we left ticking away the years in the first part of our story.

After hearing of Miss Eagle's passing, the Queen gave it to W. T. Stead, a respected newspaper editor and champion of Spiritualism, requesting him to award it to the medium he considered had accomplished most for the movement.

Return is speedy

Mr Stead, Sir William Crookes and Alfred Russel Wallace decided this should be Mrs Etta Wriedt, the American direct voice medium. The presentation was arranged.

Many years passed. In April, 1912, Mr Stead was invited to New York to speak at Carnegie Hall on the subject of world peace. He sailed on the *Titanic*.

On the night of 14 April the *Titanic* struck an iceberg.

Two days later Mrs Wriedt's control gave full details of the disaster, naming Mr Stead as one of many prominent people who went down with the 'unsinkable' ship.

The following night Mr Stead spoke, the first of many spirit communications.

Mrs Wriedt decided the watch should be returned to Britain before she passed.

One of her sitters was approached with the request to deliver it to England. This was Canadian Prime Minister Mackenzie King, a convinced Spiritualist.

He took it to the Duchess of Hamilton, who arranged for it to be housed at the London Spiritualist Alliance, now the College of Psychic Studies. Sadly the watch was stolen from their premises in 1963.

It bore the legend: 'Presented by W. T. Stead to Mrs Etta Wriedt through whose mediumship Queen Victoria's direct voice was heard in London in July 1911.'

Queen Victoria was not the only monarch to make a well-attested spirit return.

Heard in German

Her eldest son, Britain's King Edward VII, communicated to Lady Warwick, always in German.

She told *PN*'s former editor Maurice Barbanell that once, at Warwick Castle, she noticed a seance trumpet standing on the floor.

'I picked it up, and immediately I heard the voice of my old friend, King Edward, talking in German.'

At that time Mrs Wriedt was visiting the castle.

'Whenever I sat with Mrs Wriedt,' added Lady Warwick, 'I always heard King Edward's voice, always speaking in German. He was so persistent that I got no other results, so I left off sitting.'

King Edward received warning of his impending passing eighteen weeks before it occurred.

One night at dinner he turned to his neighbour, the Countess of Fingall, and told her he wanted a private word later.

After the meal, he led her to a quiet corner of the drawing room. With deep solemnity he said, 'Lady Fingall, your friend Mrs Jameson has hurt me very badly.'

Mrs Jameson, a sister of Earl Haig, often received messages from her 'dead' brother, George, via automatic writing.

The King told Lady Fingall, 'She knows how much I loved my sister. She has written to me giving a message, which she says is from Alice.'

The King repeated the communication, 'The time is short. You must prepare.'

The startled Lady Fingall, realizing the message's meaning, asked if there were any proof that it came from Princess Alice.

'Yes,' replied King Edward. 'She said I was to remember a day when we were on Ben Nevis together, found white heather and divided it.'

He could see no way in which Mrs Jameson might have learned of this incident.

Not long before Edward's passing in 1910, his wife, Alexandra, invited a London medium to Windsor. Unknown to the King, a seance was held in one of the castle ante-rooms.

A dozen sitters heard remarkable messages. One foretold the early death of the king in the house of his birth, and the outbreak in a few years of a great war.

When the Queen was holidaying in Corfu the following year, she was told Edward was not feeling well. Despite being reassured his condition was not in the least serious, she immediately left for home.

Alexandra arrived at Buckingham Palace – the King's birthplace – in time to see her husband breathe his last.

And she lived to see the First World War. She passed in 1925. No psychic story about Royalty would be complete without reference to King George V.

One spring morning in 1881, deckhands on HMS *Bacchante* were enjoying the calm seas. Suddenly, about 200 yards away, bathed in a red glow, they saw a phantom brig sailing towards them.

The startled officer of the watch believed a collision was iminent. Yet, as he stared, the mysterious brig vanished as suddenly as it had come.

The incident was recorded in the ship's log.

Soon a knock was heard at the captain's door. A young cadet asked permission to copy the log entry into his diary.

This cadet was the future King George V.

Thanked by a king

The monarch was no stranger to psychic happenings.
When a *PN* reader forwarded a spirit message from his
mother, Queen Alexandra, he was surprised to receive a
personally-written letter of thanks signed by the king.

Addressed from Buckingham Palace and dated 6 February, 1935, it read:

'It was so very kind of you to send me such an inspiring
message from my dear mother.

I fully understand what she has thought fit to convey to
me through your instrumentality.

I also thank you for the enclosed, viz, *Psychic News*,
which I shall certainly peruse with pleasure.

Guided from Beyond

My mother is constantly with me, watching and guiding
my private affairs.

I appreciate her message about a dark cloud shadowing
the home, but a happy reunion in the land of eternal
sunshine.'

Less than a year later, George V passed on.

A curious spirit message concerning the king once came
in unusual circumstances.

Mrs M Gordon-Moore, a well-known Spiritualist and
noted London hostess, wrote an account in her book,
Things I Can't Explain.

Early in March, 1935, a messenger arrived at Mrs
Gordon-Moore's home. He told her maid he was com-
manded to wait for a reply.

Mrs Gordon-Moore wrote, 'I opened the note, and to
my surprise it was an urgent request to go to a well-known
London club to meet a Member of Parliament and his wife,
neither of whom I knew, at 11 o'clock the next morning.
The note was from a man we had met several times and
liked.'

She showed it to her husband and asked if he would
accompany her.

The couple set off the following morning.

At first they saw no one in the club room.

Then Mrs Gordon-Moore made out 'the figure of a tall, practical-looking woman in country clothes standing at the side of a heavily curtained window'.

She asked the woman if she knew Mrs Q, the writer of the note.

Looking relieved, she said quickly, 'Oh, you must be Mrs Gordon-Moore. Mr Q and my husband will be here in a moment.'

The two men arrived as she spoke, apologizing for the mysterious summons and expressing their thanks. Though their manner was charming, they appeared to find some difficulty in revealing their mission.

The tall woman's husband began, 'I – er – we heard from Mr Q that you might be able to help us in a rather unusual matter.'

He hesitated. Mrs Gordon-Moore gently asked in what way she could be of use.

'It may seem very odd,' the man replied, 'but we believe you understand messages from the unseen. You do, don't you?'

'Yes, I do,' she answered.

'Well,' he continued, 'we want someone to give a message and thought perhaps you, understanding these things, could do this for us.'

Mystified, the hearer commented, 'Surely you could do this yourselves much better than I or anyone.'

'No, we want a direct secret message given. It is urgent. Our name must not appear for obvious reasons and we do not want it broadcast. It must be a strictly private message.'

Mrs Gordon-Moore asked, 'Who must be told?'

'One of the King's younger sons,' came the surprising response. 'Could you do this?'

Mrs Gordon-Moore said she did not think it was possible, but asked for the message.

Both the man and his wife looked worried. After a few moments' silence the husband said quietly, 'We trust you. I know we can. This is the message. "The king is going to die very soon. There may be confusion and danger. A younger son will succeed and should be prepared".'

Mrs Gordon-Moore was astounded. 'Surely the Prince of Wales will succeed when the time comes?' she said.

'No!' she was told. 'He won't succeed. He will disappear and a young son will reign.'

Mrs Gordon-Moore asked how these details were known. The tall woman, she was told, had suddenly become entranced for the first time some weeks ago.

The controlling spirit entity repeated the same message, again and again over the next days until the bemused couple decided to try to find a means of delivering it.

Mrs Gordon-Moore knew that if she delivered the message in the King's lifetime, it would cause distress and anxiety to many people.

Reluctantly, the couple agreed nothing further should be done.

Medium Leslie Flint described one of his most dramatic independent voice seances in his book, *Voices in the Dark*.

Noting that two sitters had booked in as Mrs Brown and Miss Smith, Leslie felt they could have shown more imagination in their choice of pseudonyms.

'This blatancy made the ladies' suspicions of me very obvious,' he wrote. Many sitters 'made it abundantly clear their only purpose in sitting with me was to find out what trick I employed to produce the voices.'

At this seance, one communicator announced himself as Alec Holden. An animated conversation ensued between the communicator and his widow, one of the two women.

He intimated that she and her friend had held unspecified positions of great trust.

Then the group heard an elderly man's voice, at first indistinct. When it became clear, the two incognito sitters' spontaneous reaction was to rise and curtsey to their 'dead' monarch.

Voice is recognized

After the sitting, Mrs Holden revealed she and her friend had been attached for many years to the royal household. The unmistakable voice was that of King George V.

Journalist and pioneer Spiritualist Hannen Swaffer once met King George II of Greece at the opening of Estelle Roberts' psychic centre in Wimbledon, South-west London.

The Greek monarch revealed, 'I have myself given your King (this was George V) spirit messages.'

In more recent years, after the uncrowned Edward VIII abdicated, his younger brother succeeded to the throne, taking the title George VI.

His retiring personality seemed ill-suited to the rigours of kingship. One great handicap was a distressing stammer. After doctors had failed to cure this, a speech therapist was called in. With his help, and the loving, steadfast support of Queen Elizabeth, now the Queen Mother, George VI became one of Britain's best-loved monarchs.

The royal couple's bravery and devotion to duty during the difficult years of the Second World War won them a special place in the hearts of their subjects.

Lionel Logue, the Australian 'voice doctor' became a close friend of the king. He happened to be a Spiritualist, and passed to the monarch many spirit messages received through the mediumship of Lilian Bailey.

These were always accepted.

When the therapist's beloved wife passed in 1945, Hannen Swaffer did his utmost to comfort the bereaved man. He arranged a sitting with Lilian, giving her no clue to the sitter's identity.

The King's treatment was confidential, and no press photographs of the therapist had appeared.

As soon as the seance began, even before she became entranced, the medium turned to her sitter with some embarrassment.

'I don't know why it is, and I scarcely like to tell you,' she murmured, 'but George V is here. He asks me to thank you for what you did for his son.'

This statement made a deep impression on the Australian.

At his second sitting, in Hannen Swaffer's flat, he received survival evidence that completely convinced him.

Lilian's guide asked if he had any questions he would like to ask.

The speech therapist parried with the question, 'Does my wife want to say anything about the place where we first met?'

The guide appeared puzzled when he relayed the dead wife's reply. It was, 'She is referring to a bird named Charlie. It is not a canary. It looks like a sparrow.'

The Australian was overwhelmed. It was at his best friend, Charlie Sparrow's, birthday party he met and fell in love with the future Mrs Logue.

'Does she remember the place?' asked the Australian.

'It was Free . . . Fremantle,' transmitted the guide.

This was correct. The speech therapist was so impressed that he rushed off to Buckingham Palace to tell the king.

Lionel Logue once told Lilian that Spiritualism had transformed his life and enabled him to understand his work.

Correcting speech defects occupied the major part of his life.

Lionel Logue told the medium he had been guided to leave Australia when there was no apparent reason. Without knowing why, he sold his home and emigrated to Britain, where he had no prospects.

Through later seances, Lionel Logue realized he had come to London to cure the grave speech defect of the man destined to be King.

The therapist was probably a natural psychic. He instantly knew what was wrong with his new patients.

Shortly after his passing, George VI used Lilian's mediumship to speak to his Australian friend.

Lionel Logue was always grateful to the medium for the comfort and survival proof she offered. He became god-father to her eldest grandson. And in his will he left Lilian a very special chair – the one used by George VI when he attended the speech therapy treatments. The Queen Mother's youngest brother, David Bowes-Lyon, showed evidence of clairvoyance in boyhood. When the War Office reported his brother Michael missing during World War I, David refused to wear mourning. For he had 'seen' Michael twice.

His head was bandaged. Michael was very ill and appeared in a large house surrounded by fir trees.

Months later David was proved correct. News eventually came that Michael, wounded in the head, was in a German prison hospital.

Glamis Castle, the Queen Mother's family seat, is traditionally haunted. David reported seeing ghosts, whom he called the 'grey people'. He was able to describe their costumes in detail.

Sandringham is said to have a poltergeist. Windsor's ghostly royal visitors include Henry VIII, Elizabeth I, Charles I and George II.

In 1968 the present Queen was reported to have spotted John Brown, her ancestor Victoria's psychic ghillie, at Balmoral.

And Victoria herself has apparently appeared in the grounds of her former Isle of Wight home, Osborne House.

Services recognized

Buckingham Palace has the reported earthbound figure of Major John Gwynne, a private secretary in Edward VII's household, who committed suicide after a divorce action.

Several Royal Family members have received psychic healing. Harry Edwards always refused to reveal publicly the identities of royalty whom he treated, with the exception of Princess Marie Louise, great-aunt of the Queen.

His services to the princess were officially recognized when the Lord Chamberlain invited him to attend her funeral at St George's Chapel, Windsor.

And the proud father, the Prince of Wales, is on record as saying in an address on the futility of orthodox religious dogma that to him it was more important for people to be 'given an awareness of the things of the spirit and of the meaning and infinite beauty of nature.'

Copyright *Psychic News*, July 1982.

3

Reincarnation ☆ Guides ☆ Healing

At some point along the way, be it a public demonstration of clairvoyance or a private consultation, mention will be made of past lives, guides and healing. These three subjects are part and parcel of the whole area of Spiritual and psychic activity. I have therefore invited a healer and Spiritual philosopher to answer some questions aimed directly at these controversial subjects.

Your guru (and mine) for this particular stage of the journey will be Samantha. Over the past eighteen months, I have received a steady stream of correspondence from her, on all manner of subjects related to the Spiritual and psychic. Not only have I been provided with some unique insights but I have also received some extremely accurate and interesting clairvoyant readings.

Samantha became a Licentiate of Psychic Science in the '50s and she also holds an honorary PhD. Her lifestyle is simple and spartan, partly through choice and partly through circumstance. She prefers to lead an almost recluse-like existence, seeing only those who need healing and counsel.

Her life ambition and hope is to have her own healing sanctuary. She has no idea at present how she will surmount the material obstacles that such a project presents – she just puts faith in her spiritual mission – plus a little help from her guides.

This chapter is her contribution to the *Directory*, for which I thank her.

Reincarnation

Q: As a Spiritual philosopher, you hold some deep convictions, perhaps one should say insights, about reincarnation. In this context, can you say where we are likely to be going on the evolutionary path, or put another way, what is our spiritual destination?

A: After over thirty years of study on matters psychic and Spiritual, I have reached the conclusion, which accords with all forms of teaching on reincarnation, that we are evolving miniature gods in our own right.

For the earnest seeker who applies himself to attending lectures and reading all the subject material, an overall picture will soon emerge to fortify the theory of reincarnation. Much proof is also being found in the new psycho-expansion groups where the super-conscious mind (not the subconscious) is being released through relaxation techniques.

When we have lived through every aspect of the human life, experiencing every emotion, hardship and happiness, we reach the stage of moving up to the next classroom as it were, which is a dimension of consciousness existing outside the physical rate of vibration, and so hidden from us until we reach our own particular perfection.

Between rebirths, we spend periods of rest in what are known as the astral planes, and maybe the lower spiritual level. Our true work of entering the finishing school and becoming the god-like entity, which is our true destiny, will not actually commence until we have graduated finally from the dreary round of continual rebirth.

The graduation of the entity will be marked by a change of form. As we progress, we will eventually outgrow the need for any recognizable shape but will exist merely in the form of pure light. This will be to do with the stepping-up of our rate of vibration. This does not mean, however, that we shall ever lose our personal identity. This will stay with us for as long as we wish. Only when we have finished our work (in the spiritual planes) of helping to create other worlds and other humanities, will we wish to join entirely with the Source of all life, wherein lies the nirvanah, as the Hindus refer to the state of perfect bliss.

The way is far from easy, for the seekers will get no special privileges in this world: in fact, he or she is all the more ready to shoulder the responsibilities which others shrug off, for they know that by facing their destiny, they are getting the lessons of this life over quickly in order to enter the realms of peace and happiness.

In a nutshell, the answer to where we are going is that we are evolving to become gods and creators. When we pass our final goal, we will blend once more into the body of God, which can only be described to our earthly senses as the source of all energy, intelligence and love, qualities which are evident in a shadowy kind of way in human life at its very best.

Q: What laws govern our rate of spiritual progress?

A: The laws which govern our rate of spiritual progress are those laws which have been taught by such masters as Jesus of Nazareth, Krishna and Buddha. They taught us to love our neighbour, help the poor and the weak, harm no man or woman nor the animals who are defenceless. Buddha put it in a way which we can all understand without any need to study religious law. He stated that we should aspire to right thinking, right living and the quality of compassion.

There is absolutely no excuse whatsoever for anyone, whether they have heard the word of God spoken or not, to neglect their spiritual progress, for we all have the voice within us which tells us when we are committing an unworthy act – this is not necessarily when we offend some silly rule of society or indulge in a little strong drink etc. We all know, though, when and if our particular actions will harm others. This IS sin. The adulterer thinks he will not be found out, so what harm, he reasons? The harm is obvious when his wife feels betrayed after giving him perfect loyalty. He has harmed her and the devastating emotional hurt is caused by his sin.

For every mean act that we commit, our spiritual progress is halted and, likewise, for every act of self-sacrifice that we aspire to, we take a step up in our spiritual progress. The law is to overcome the selfishness of our ego. Each time that we quiet the desires of an ego which produces greed, negativity, cruelty etc, and rise above these desires, so we rise to better spiritual levels.

It is not always obvious to us on the surface that we are rising in our soul state. We eventually find though that if we are truly sincere, guidance will be given. If we need help to be strong, prayer will bring us the strength to do that which is right, even though we may have faint hearts and doubts.

As we aspire to become more spiritual, the actual atomic structure of our body becomes slightly more rarefied. Many people become alarmed when they find that they may not feel the same animal-type strength which they formally possessed. We have all met the nuns who have a positively ethereal look in their faces, and although most of these nuns are kept pretty healthy by the spartan life, they do imperceptibly draw away from the animal strength level, and this can sometimes be seen in their physical appearance.

The actual law governing spiritual progress, is that we are literally given the inner power to overcome self (the ego) so that our soul can guide us in our actions, rather than our human personality – if we allow it to do so! There is no other way to spiritual progress; no priest can take our sins and thereby make a jot of difference to our spiritual level by forgiving us our sins. It is up to us to do this by trying sincerely to right the wrong that we have done. If this is not possible, then we must find some way to perform an act of self-sacrifice that will outweigh the selfish or cruel act which was our sin.

An unknown Maori once wrote a beautiful poem in which he stated the truism: 'You are your own devil, you are your own god, you fashioned the path, that your footsteps have trod.' He was referring to the judgement day which we go through, not once as some suppose, but the judgement day which will occur after each and every physical death, when we shall then stand in the astral plane, revealing our spiritual state by our lights and the colours of our auras. We shall also be shown our earthly existences, indicating where we failed and where we succeeded, for we take along with us a microdot of pure energy which contains a record of everything we have ever said or done in our earthly sojourns.

The Creator endowed us with the power and the intelligence to be responsible for our own spiritual evolution. He is not a vengeful old man sitting in the sky, waiting to cast sinners into the fiery pit. The hell we experience is to stand and judge what we have been on earth – and we judge ourselves from the light of pure crystal-clear spiritual reasoning which is reality in its essence. On earth, we cloud our spiritual judgement of ourselves because of our animal instincts. No one will blame us for our faults, for the higher guides know that we are evolving entities, and we shall make mistakes until we reach true realization.

With each incarnation, our inner knowing will be stronger, so there is no excuse for anyone to say that they never had the same chance as their brother or sister. We have all lived many times, and it is up to us entirely how we progress or regress spiritually.

Q: How is our sex, race, religion and nationality determined?

A: When in the astral dimension between incarnations, we know (with the help of our guides) what environmental factor is needed, consequently such matters as sex, race, religion and nationality are decided upon in the light of what different set of experiences are required from those recently lived through. A conference takes place, and the returning soul states what he or she thinks could prove the most useful and helpful setting. Consent is given and the process begins of guiding the entity (you and I) towards the foetus of an unborn child – in a setting in which we feel we are lacking in knowledge.

I have known a schoolteacher in this life, who experienced under regression (the higher awareness state induced for reviewing past lives), a period when she worked as a guide in the lower spiritual realms. Her main task was guiding souls to their places of reincarnation back on earth. She described this experience as very illuminating. To her, it was like standing at a spot which was a junction of several passages, similar to those in the Underground or a subway – and there were literally hundreds of souls rushing along these passageways. She had to point the path out for those who were uncertain of which direction to take. This was a particularly interesting account because the question had often been discussed (and still is) in Spiritualist circles, as to whether those who have worked as guides ever return to earth.

Q: If our sex can change from life to life, could this factor ever lead to sexual disorientation or confusion?

A: Having thoughtfully considered this question, I would say the answer is NO. There are many who believe that this factor can cause confusion, thinking perhaps that by switching causes, there is a tendency for humans to become homosexual.

I consider that this is most unlikely, for our sexual maturity is covered mainly by our genetic coding. The instincts and traits that we bring with us from other lives are spiritual. They would be mainly whether we are selfish or whether we help people. These spiritual instincts would also cover the creative gifts such as painting and writing – and the ability to appreciate beauty.

I rather think that sexual aberrations are those arising from purely mental and physical causes with damage to the genes in very rare cases. I cannot honestly think that humans would be penalized for carrying memory motivations from a former opposite sex existence. There would be far too much confusion about the procreation of the human race, were we to be burdened in this way. I have never known of anyone being handicapped by a former opposite sex existence, although I have heard some males claim that they strayed from the norm because they had been told that they were women in their former lives!

I have been allowed to experience the memory of inhabiting a former male body of my own on at least two occasions. These observations had no emotional effect on me at all. My mood was one of clinical detachment, which allows me to come to the conclusion that our super-conscious memories are objective in order that we can keep a record of our progress.

Q: Apart from the usual associations that are formed during a life, close and often very intense emotional-sexual relationships are formed that may not last a lifetime but they can certainly leave a traumatic mark for life. Can such relationships be explained by past life association?

A: The answer to this could quite probably be YES. There is a wealth of written documentation on the subject, where the people concerned, sometimes serious researchers with scientific and medical backgrounds, have declared that someone in their lives has been a close associate, not once but during many lifetimes. During research via meditation and deep relaxation, they experience 'far memory' flashes, where the person they are close to in this life is seen as a son, daughter, wife or husband or close friend from some period in the past.

The most written about example is by Dr Guirdam who has written such books as *The Lake and the Castle*. Dr Guirdam claims that he is associated with a group of people who were also members of the Cathar sect in the Middle

Ages, and there is some very convincing evidence put forward to support his theory.

Many of us have experienced that chance meeting with someone of the opposite sex and we know in some uncanny way that this is not just another brief social encounter. We may move on immediately but the encounter will occupy our thoughts again and again, the impact being felt for some time to come. Coupled with this will be a regret that we did not pause a little longer and become better acquainted. I believe that this happens to people at least once or twice in their lives.

For the not-so-brief encounter, I have heard people say that it was though a spark flashed between their eyes. They find difficulty in describing what was obviously a merging of spiritual energies. In extreme cases some very happily married women have allowed themselves to be approached and before twenty-four hours have passed, both are so emotionally committed that all considerations are set at nil against a power which is holding them in its grip. Secret meetings are followed by divorce and their friends and acquaintances mutter about 'going off the rails'. The victims of this overwhelming attraction are powerless to help themselves or be 'sensible', as society would say.

I feel that this instant recognition is where the two people in love have reincarnated at the same time into a geographical location where they are likely to meet. They were probably lovers or husband and wife in a former existence. Their love is at the spiritual depth, so the question of resisting mere physical attraction is not the case. It is unfortunate when incidents like this wreak havoc with the lives of those who are happily married – or have been – but perhaps this is yet another case of being tested! If the man or woman could resist the overwhelming longing to be with their new love (or old love), would this have been a great leap forward spiritually? It is very difficult to decide such a question and, once again, the decision must be made by the individual. This sort of situation could be the case where someone had to prove their love to someone whose heart he or she broke in a previous existence. There are many paths along which one may consider the possibilities, but one thing that I say for certain, these are two very old souls reuniting for perhaps centuries. The recognition and attraction is still there at the depth of their souls, if not their physical memory.

Q: What circumstances govern the period of time spent between incarnations?

A: There are many theories and I do not think that there is any hard and fast rule. I feel that it would depend mainly on what kind of life the subject had experienced in his or her last earthly life. If it had been a very stressful existence, the entity would be allowed a longer time to 'rest' in the other dimension. The period of time would therefore be less for someone who had lived a fairly comfortable life with not too much illness or stress and strain.

It is not so much the physical aspect of the prior incarnation which necessitates a rest, but extreme unhappiness which causes wounds to the soul. Emotional rather than physical wounds would have a far more devastating effect on the spirit, so some need a longer rest in the spirit world, to prepare once again for the battleground which we call life.

For anyone who doubts that we are going through a life which causes great suffering to our spirit, let me say that there have been thousands of recorded cases of people being resuscitated in hospitals after they had briefly experienced clinical death. They all report having been with wonderful companions in such a beautiful place that they pleaded not to be sent back to a human existence. But of course, if an entity has not finished the lessons of this life, then a return for the allotted period of time is inevitable. This is an irreversible law.

Another reason for a longer interim period would be the need to wait for exactly the right opportunity to be born into a certain family, where the lessons still to be learned can most suitably by taught.

Those who have specially trained themselves to retain

conscious memory of higher dimension experiences, report being witness to entities refusing to return to earth. In such cases, these entities are 'booted' back to the waiting embryos. This is not quite as cruel as it may seem, for the guides have a complete record of all that has happened to a particular entity since it first opened its eyes as a human baby, way back in the days when man first made his bow. The guides will know exactly what qualities the entity lacks, and his next incarnation will be chosen on the basis of purely logical selection. There is never any thought of punishment being meted out to the entity, but if this person has caused pain and suffering, then there is a possibility that he or she will be born to become a victim of such suffering, for this is karmic law.

Many schools of religious thought believe that this is so. The law of karma does seem to be the only theory which makes complete sense. If mankind became enlightened to a much higher degree, then life itself would not be so full of grief and woe and reincarnating would not be such an ordeal. We must continue to live grief and heartaches over and over again, in life after life, until man learns the essential lessons that are put before him.

Q: Does the reincarnated spirit represent the whole or only part of a higher self which exists permanently in the spirit realm?

A: This is the 64,000 dollar question. Some researchers believe that our oversoul remains in the spirit world, whilst we live out our puny little earth life. In the meantime, the oversoul is supposed to be sending down all sorts of wisdom to help us from the upper realms.

I do not go along with this theory because of my own experiences. I feel that we can carry on our normal work while our spirit half is engaged in work elsewhere. The masters of the East demonstrate this daily. I believe that our higher spirit is with us here and now, and when we request enlightened information via meditation, we either receive it from a present stock of information, or the higher self detaches from the body to enquire in the higher dimension. Therefore, in the latter instance, although the information is coming from the other dimension, our spirit will be back with us as soon as we have 'got the message', for the spirit moves at instantaneous speed – unlike our physical body which has to travel through dense matter in an equally dense form.

Our wisdom is not stored with some spirit form in the heavenly realms, it is here with us. Our spirit self only travels off on the odd occasion, an example of which I have given.

Now let me give a word of warning! There are some types of mental illness which result from the doorway being open by accident. The victim of the 'open doorway' condition is aware of other scenes and people with whom he or she is conversing – people who are not visible in the physical realm. Those around the sufferer think that the person is ill, which in a sense is true. This kind of illness can result when a person has strong and natural medium-istic tendencies which have not been properly developed as a secondary aspect of the mind – secondary in the sense that it in no way interferes with the everyday thought and action processes. Often, the confused state is merely a temporary condition which will pass with rest and freedom from everyday pressures. The problem can be made worse, though, by doctors who administer drug treatments. Doctors are often unware of the true cause of the condition and will look for a purely physical cause.

This illness also illustrates just one of the dangers of trying to rush psychic development. No psychic development should ever be forced. Psychic abilities must develop naturally with the aid of quiet relaxation and placing the mind on higher beautiful thoughts. The threshold will then come under full control.

Q: If we accept the theory of reincarnation, it would seem that we are responsible for own destinies according to the laws of karma. What advice can you give to those of us who wish to improve our spiritual path of progress?

A: The first and paramount point to realize as soon as we are old enough to distinguish between right and wrong, is that we must listen to the voice within. That voice guides each and every one of us throughout our lives. It means learning to let our deeper conscience be our guide.

All of us, at one time or another, have had to make important decisions affecting our lives and the lives of those close to us. We have to do much SOUL searching, to know where necessity calls for us to carry out actions which in the process will upset others. If we arrive at a decision which will adversely affect others, we should then sit quietly and relax, freeing our mind from the 'logical' working of our thought processes. If we then really listen, another 'voice' will take over and we may well be shocked when the voice tells us that we have made the wrong decision.

This inner intuition is the voice of our spirit, which knows the result of any action that we take. Ultimately, that action will be right or wrong for our karma or for the karma of any other person involved. When we stifle the inner voice, we usually fall flat on our face. How often have you heard a person say, 'I somehow knew deep inside me that I was making a mistake. How I wish I had listened to my intuition, then I wouldn't have come such a cropper.' It has happened to me more than once, but luckily I have learned at long last to let my inner voice have the final word. It really does pay to listen to the inner spirit. Not only can we help ourselves by taking heed but we can also help others, particularly when they are unable to face the stress of a difficult situation. The power we have to help ourselves will work for another if we make a mental request. Let me add, though, that we are not always allowed to take the weight off the shoulders of another, for it may be their karmic duty to face things alone.

To progress – SERVE your fellow man in any little way that you can, even if this means that you sometimes give up your own ease and comfort. Every time that you share a burden from the goodness of your heart, freely and without any thought of reward or egotistical display, you

46

have earned yourself an excellent mark in your karmic record book.

The choice of progression or regression is yours. It will be no good complaining afterwards that you had no choice but to commit a mean act, for we judge ourselves later through the reality of our spiritual eyes.

Guides

Q: Of all the subjects that are discussed in relation to the Spiritual and psychic, less is mentioned about spirit guides in comparison to other areas of activity. Guides just seem to be accepted without too much comment. Can you tell us a little more about guides?

A: The guides that mediums refer to are usually discarnates who have lived the earth life themselves and who have progressed to the lower spiritual planes. Everyone on this level performs a work of service of some kind. There are spirits who look after those who reach the spirit world in an exhausted state, perhaps having suffered a lingering and painful terminal illness, or those political prisoners who have been tortured to death. Some spirits look after suicides. These unfortunates are a special case and they need much help to come out of the darkness in which they are enveloped.

It is questionable as to whether guides train in *all* services to mankind. Guides are not very prone to talking about themselves. Usually, though, those that we call guides are the discarnates who communicate with us here. They give assistance by helping people along the path of progress. This assistance is given by leading lives in certain directions. Guides communicate with mediums who are used to relay messages from the spirit world. As a rule, these messages are from deceased relatives, but sometimes they can also be a message of comfort from the guide to an individual who has been through a rather bad time. The guide will often give a date in the future for a considerable improvement in the individual's affairs. In fact, it is safe to say that there have been many cases where a message of hope from a guide has deterred someone from committing suicide or relieved a deep depression.

This is the type of guide that we hear most about in the world of Spiritualism. There are more evolved guides who dwell in the higher planes of the spirit world. These spirits are referred to as guides from the upper realms. These souls are highly evolved and shine with such a brilliance that the human eye is bedazzled by their appearance. It is a fact that as a spirit progresses, more cosmic light is absorbed into the spirit form. Some upper realms guides shine with such a brilliance that they have to cloak themselves in a form of energy plasma that dims their brilliance, otherwise the human eye would be blinded by the concentration of light when they appear before us. I have been in the presence of one of these 'shining' souls and the light that surrounded the figure was as intense as half a dozen searchlights in a darkened room. I was forced to shield my eyes from the intensity of the glare.

Many more people than would care to admit it have seen 'the light' and the figure that it surrounds. They are often afraid that their friends will think them unbalanced if they admit to such an experience. For most people this would be a once in a lifetime experience, but I believe that fully-fledged mediums see the upper realms guides in all their glory on more than one occasion.

If we think about this phenomenon carefully, it does give us a clue to our own nature – that we are entities composed of an energy that is indestructible – just like those beings in science-fiction films. The guides can make themselves visible to us or they can contact us as invisible messengers. Fortunately for us, the upper realms guides, indeed all the guides who aid humanity, are of a benevolent nature. There is another type of entity who belongs to the obverse side of the spiritual realm – from the plane we refer to as hell – but we are not concerned here with this kind of entity, except to say that in no way could that type of entity become a guide.

From the case I quoted earlier, it appears that we can act as guides in the spiritual realms, and then still return to this existence. The lady I mentioned was able to review her past lives and 'saw' herself as a guide in the spiritual realm and, of course, she was reborn into her present life here.

The average guide is at a slightly higher stage of progression than the average individual here on earth. Their advantage is possession of a much wider spiritual awareness, coupled with the fact that they have access to knowledge about us that we do not even have ourselves.

Q: What reason is there for particular guides choosing to assist us on our journey through life?

A: Certain guides see that they have the necessary know-how that will suit our particular requirements and personality – and another important factor is our stage of spiritual progress. The lower our position on the ladder of progress, the less-skilled would be the guide, in the same way that a university don would not be teaching pupils in the infant class.

This is my belief and I am sure that there are other factors involved too. One of my guides is a gypsy girl who lived in Canada during the last century. She led a nomadic life and suffered many hardships. Considering my own hardships in this life, she is probably best suited as the one who would know my thoughts and feelings to the letter. She is well qualified to advise and encourage me when I need advice and encouragement.

Q: Can we attract the attention of our guide or guides during a crisis or when we need assistance?

A: We can call them to us if we are in an emergency situation. Once, when travelling, I suffered a badly gashed leg in an accident. The flesh was open to the bone and the pain was excruciating. I quickly called on my healing guides to help and no sooner had I asked than the pain began to subside. Within twenty to thirty minutes the flesh had begun to knit together. I had no opportunity at the time to bathe the dirt out of the wound but I never suffered an infection and the wound healed beautifully. Today I bear only the faintest scar.

On another occasion, I received a nasty steam scalding. Once again I quickly called for my guides to help. Again the pain soon subsided and the skin bore no mark of blistering or peeling, although the skin surface did remain red for a time. As we know, cures can be effected by self-hypnosis – but I do not think that I could have managed self-hypnosis under those circumstances!

Harry Edwards, the late President of the National Federation of Spiritual Healers, also had a car accident, and just like myself, he called on his guides to heal a gashed leg, and just like me, his wound responded in a similar manner – it healed within a very short space of time.

These examples are of guides called in emergencies, normally we should sit quietly and attune ourselves to the guides by deep relaxation, at the same time sending out thoughts for help. Under these conditions, the guide will usually come softly and unobtrusively to our side.

Guides often come to us unasked. We may feel a prod in the shoulder or they may grasp an arm to make their presence known – usually when we are engrossed in material pursuits and unaware of them. I am not too sure how they achieve this touching effect. It may be through a concentration of energy or projecting thoughts to us so that we sense a touch on the arm etc.

One does not have to have mediumistic tendencies to receive these impressions because many ordinary people will get these odd sensations.

When we as healers attune to begin a healing session, the guides automatically know and they will position themselves near us to aid in the healing of a patient. I once 'saw' a pair of hands working on a lady's spine. The phantom hands were working in the space between my own hands which were resting on the patient's spine. I realized by the robe that rested on the wrists of this guide, that it was my Chinese guide. The patient of course could not see these hands, for I was in what is known as a heightened state of awareness, as all healers are, or should be, when working.

I would say in answer to the question that guides will come just at a thought from us – which is as good as a telegram in the spirit world.

Thought has tremendous power and reality in its own right. We do not fully realize this in the physical world, although parapsychology researchers are beginning to take note that we are aware of one another's thoughts on the human existence level.

Q: How do guides influence our actions?

A: They influence us through our thought processes. Most of us will sit quietly when we wish to do some serious thinking and planning. It is at this time, when we take a break from the hurly-burly of life, that the guides will be sending thoughts and promptings to superimpose over our own thought processes. Let me add that they do not usually interfere with our thoughts unless it is an issue which is very important for our own good.

Guides can also benefit us in other ways, by influencing the thoughts of those closest to us. This may be in business, or in affairs of the heart, or in any number of ways.

When the guides consider that a person (or cause) needs and is deserving of help, they will go to the corners of the earth to attempt to 'pull strings' to get it. That assistance may not be in the form of some gigantic cash offering, but it will be practical. For example, it might be help for someone who has tried desperately hard to get a job – someone who has always put themselves out for others with no thought of return.

I can mention one particular case that I know of, where a woman was left with five children to feed, not knowing where the next penny was coming from. This situation was not her fault and had come about through a set of unfortunate circumstances. The mother prayed on her knees to God, asking for just enough money to buy food for the children – she did not even include herself in her prayer. She then went out of the house, still in a mood of hopelessness but secretly wishing for a miracle to happen. The miracle did happen and the money appeared from a friend who happened to be in the same street at the same time that the woman walked out of her house.

So many things happen, of which we say, 'It was like a miracle'. Not a miracle – just the subtle way in which the guides carry out their good works, often in answer to prayer – but not selfish prayer. Most wise people will add to their prayer, 'if it be thy will'. That is precisely the kind of prayer that is usually answered, for by no means will the guides automatically answer the demanding kind of supplication. They realize that this is not good for the person who says such prayers.

Q: If we fail in our earthly mission, for example by putting too much emphasis on the material rather than the spiritual, do our guides suffer as a consequence of our failure?

A: There is a short sharp answer to this – YES! But this is only in the same sense that one would feel sad for an erring child who has fooled around in school. The goal of the guide is to see how far the person in his charge can progress spiritually. The gaining of material wealth has little to do with the reason for incarnating, although we should all earn our daily bread as part of life in a normal and ordered society. It is selfish to lean on others to provide for us, at the same time it is spiritually retrogressive to grab more than your fair share at the expense of others.

There is very little more to say on this question.

Q: Can you communicate with your own guides at will?

A: At times yes. I am not on nodding terms with them so to speak, but they are always present with me when I am doing my healing work. On other occasions, if I make a special effort, they will show themselves to me but most of the time they remain unseen. In the sleep state it is different, I actually talk and walk with them occasionally because I am in the spirit body and communication is of course much easier.

No doubt I could talk constantly with my guides if I trained intensely, but I have always tried to practise what I preach – and that is to let development come naturally. On occasion I have made a special effort, as I once did for a special healing session. This particular case was very sad and I prayed for extra power. Just before I fell asleep that night, I left my physical body and glided swiftly along a pathway to what appeared to be an old Eastern city. I was partly conscious during this journey and there was a lot more to the sequence of events than can be told here. Let me just say though, that as I approached the gates of the city, I was met by many guides who came to greet me. As they led me through the gates of the city, which had a luminous green glow overhead, I lost consciousness. The reason, I suspect, is that I was not allowed to bring back knowledge of what I had seen and heard. I have since learned that this particular city is on the fifth plane in the spiritual realm.

Q: Are we likely to meet our guides when we finally enter the spirit realm?

A: We most certainly shall. They will be there to greet us like old friends, or at least those of them who have not passed on to the higher realms, though I think it more likely that we shall be allowed to visit them to give them thanks for the work they have done for us.

My first guide was the good old-fashioned guide that nearly everyone acquires. He was an American Indian and a hunter when he roamed the earth. He left me and passed to another realm some years ago. Before he moved on, he left me in the care of another guide. He also appeared to me whilst I was in conscious meditation and showed me a scene from his life as an Indian hunter. As he finally left, there were no farewell waves or dramatics, he merely conveyed to me that I would be in the care of others from that time on. Anyway, we all meet our present guides when we are in the sleep state.

Healing

Q: As a healer, can you tell us about the source of your healing power?

A: The source of healing power is the source of all natural life. When we speak of healing power, it merely means that healers have altered their state of consciousness and consequently attract larger measures of what could be termed cosmic light (transformed in some measure) to the aura or electrical fields of the patients' bodies.

There is no mystery about how science would describe this process. We receive and re-issue ultra-violet and infra-red rays, plus sub-sonic resonance and high frequency sound waves. The great mystery is how it is so safely controlled for healers to use, in the form in which it is presented. The answer could be that we are getting all these tremendous energies in the form of bio-plasma. This means that the energies have been transformed into another type of energy which presents no danger, and is indeed beneficial to the human body.

With healing rays, it is merely a matter of the vibration required for the healing. This is dealt with by the absorption of various colours of the spectrum, hence we say blue is a cool soothing colour, where an astringent effect is required, as in the case of fever. With rheumatism, a special heat effect is produced and I believe that red is the dominant colour.

When healers' hands are subjected to electrical photography, the resulting photos or plates indicate a corona around the perimeter of the hands. The corona is composed of multi-coloured flares which are mobile energy particles. When the healer is asked to THINK of healing someone, this corona light discharge, which has been medium stable, is disrupted and bursts into what looks like a volcanic eruption of energy and flaring light. This proves that as soon as a healer switches to the state of healing consciousness, he is absorbing and discharging cosmic light, acting as an energy transformer before transferring the healing energy to the patient who has the ability to absorb this power.

From the corona colours revealed by electrical photography, it is easy to see that the energies involved are of a multi-variant vibrational rate, for we measure vibration by its position in the electro-magnetic spectrum band, which is indicated by colours.

Light photons hit the mitochondria (casing) of the human cells, and this causes physiological changes such as excitation of the body system's enzymes.

Healing, in short, is more or less an interchange of natural radiation between two bio-organisms, for healers can heal plants and animals, as well as humans.

Q: What about long-term wear and tear on the normal body vitality of the healer?

A: With healing, the healer is drawing constantly from the source (the pool of universal energy which can never dry up) so those who feel drained at the end of a healing session are more likely to be taking on the depleted feeling from their patients; or maybe they are concentrating too hard with the physical mind, instead of merely standing back, as it were, and allowing the inner spiritual self to do all the work.

There is no wear and tear with a genuine healer, even in the long term. Healers may often appear to be drained but they are usually sensitive types who suffer more from the stresses of life, much more so than the materialist or the physical type. The masters have learned to overcome this by a daily practice of replenishing their equanimity and calm, but it is more difficult for the average healer to do this because few of us have gained supremacy over the physical, whereas the masters function more or less continuously in their 'I' which is the indestructible spirit.

Q: Do you ever experience frustration when treating the physical signs of a condition which has a psychological foundation, knowing full well that the cure really lies with the patient?

A: Quite definitely yes! We can sit for hours with a patient, trying very carefully to coax them to think in a more lateral direction, to get them out of their tunnel vision thinking. Sometimes it pays off but it is a difficult process and we have to watch for all sorts of factors. There are cases where it would be harmful to allow patients to realize with a sudden shock that they have been hiding from themselves.

Q: What healing technique do you use when dealing with such serious mental disturbances as the various forms of schizophrenia?

A: I would never attempt to try ANY counselling techniques in the case of a patient seriously ill with schizophrenia – not without full training in psychology. It is a job for the specialist. It does sometimes help to use prayer and the laying on of hands, as this does have a certain calming effect on the patient. It often allows the spirit doctors to get into fuller contact with the patient – by using us as mediators.

I was once able to cure a very bad case of depression by using absent healing – there was no contact whatsoever with the patient. Of course, I was not truly the healer, the thanks belonged to the guides who were working with me. They brought about the beneficial change in the patient's thinking.

Never would I think or feel that I have any magic cures for such conditions. There is so much involved; not only the patient's background, but also a physical cause is often partly instrumental, and it has now been found that certain people are allergic to certain foods that can cause psychological changes within hours.

The only thing that I can do is to rely on the superior wisdom of the healing guides, and even they cannot always alter these serious conditions, or else it may take a long time, even years, to get the patient back on the road to rational and healthy thinking.

Q: We are all prone to the pressures of modern life. What advice would you give to us so that we can lead a less stress-prone life?

A: The answer to this is best answered by the advice of the masters, 'KNOW THYSELF'. All our stresses and strains arise from reactions to situations and people which have past unpleasant connotations, or situations which make us feel subconsciously threatened – for example, if the man next door buys a brand new up-to-date car, we might feel irritated by this and call him a big show-off, but in so doing, we are revealing to the world at large that we have lost face. We feel inferior for not being able to produce the cash to buy an even more expensive car than our neighbour. This is nothing to be ashamed of, for we are all programmed to struggle for advancement. This is part of our evolutionary progress, for if everyone were content with their lot, the world would not have electricity and atomic power. There is an everlasting striving for better things. Being the first to produce that which is superior is a kind of status symbol – not a bad thing in itself, but it can lead to human jealousy. The obverse side of the coin is where the individual just doesn't give a damn about acclaim, the sort of person who is content with his or her intellectual or spiritual pursuits. Often the family of such a person will say, 'Pull your socks up and get us the nice things that other people have. You are downright lazy and think only of yourself.'

You have to be a virtual genius at handling others if you wish to get through life without too much aggravation. The strong-minded usually live alone, as I do.

I would sum up by saying that the solution is to be fair to others, but live your life as you please, so long as no harm is being done to others by your lifestyle.

Q: What are your views on the very controversial subjects of birth control and abortion?

A: Birth control? Fine, why let nature tell us what to do all the time? We don't simply lie down to die when we are sick, so why not prevent a baby being born when it is not right for us to have one in our particular situation.

Abortion is another matter. If the mother is irresponsible and the child would be born suffering, then I would say yes to abortion. But abortion so that someone can carelessly and constantly live a promiscuous life – absolutely not. This is a sin because it is constantly thwarting the overall plan of the Creator and nature, to keep the balance of the two sexes and to multiply the human race. We have yet to spread out to other planets and populate them . . . There are plenty of resources here to take us up until the time that day dawns.

Abortion is wrong when the motive is selfish or when the pregnancy is at an advanced stage, for it is denying a spirit its entry for reincarnation purposes.

Q: What results could be obtained, if some of our leading medical research scientists were invited to put questions to an experienced healer-medium? Do you think that they might receive some interesting answers and perhaps even a big breakthrough with medical research?

A: Healers and mediums have been questioned many times

but they cannot assist medical science too much. Such knowledge is held by the guides and not the mediums. The guides work in such advanced areas of knowledge that the information would sound nonsensical if it were to be passed on, in the same way that the early alchemists and men of letters refused to believe that the earth was round.

The short answer is that the world is not yet ready for the truth; the truth would be too dangerous a knowledge for men to possess at this time.

4

Sai Baba

During an extensive exchange of correspondence with
Samantha (see Chapter 3), the name of Sai Baba cropped
up time and again. This also coincided with some coverage
of Sai Baba in *Psychic News*. I eventually took the hint and
armed myself with two books: *Sai Baba Man of Miracles*
by Howard Murphet and *Visions of the Divine* by Eruch B
Fanibunda. Both books are available from the London Sai
Ram Centre.

Samantha had already given me a good indication of the
reported power of this Eastern mystic but I was completely
unprepared for the amazing accounts of healing, material-
ization and other miracles that are chronicled in the above-
mentioned books.

Sai Baba cannot be put into a category, nor should he
be, for the various observers who report and write about
his activities are not talking about just another guru.
Neither were those who told us about Krishna, Jesus, etc.

At first glance, it would seem that Sai Baba is out of
'reach' for the average Westerner, yet as you read more
about him, you feel that you know him very well. At that
first hint of recognition, you will know a little bit more
about Sai Baba and quite a lot more about yourself.

The following *Note on Sathya Sai Baba*, is contributed
by Ron Laing, co-author with Peggy Mason of *Sathya Sai
Baba The Embodiment of Love*. I am particularly grateful to
Mr Laing for the opportunity to include his *Note* which is
written with the authority of firsthand contact. His contribution has been written specifically for this chapter.

Note on Sathya Sai Baba

Sathya Sai Baba is certainly the twentieth century's world phenomenon. He was born in the remote village of Puttaparthi, near Bangalore in Southern India, on 23 November 1926. At the age of three his grandfather, Kondamma Raju, referred to him as the 'Little Master', and at the age of five he was known in the village as a Brahmanjnani (an incarnation of God).

At six he was performing miracles, materializing food, pencils, india-rubbers and notebooks for his school friends, as well as a variety of fruits from the branches of a tamarind tree which grows at the top of a hill abutting on Puttaparthi. This was in no way due to yogic powers which can be arduously learned over a period of time by sages and gurus, but through his *sankalpa* (divine will). He came into incarnation with all knowledge intact, that is to say with the sixteen *gunas* or attributes of full Divinity.

As he says: 'I am no seeker, sage or spiritual aspirant. I do not meditate on anything at all. What I *will* happens.'

At the age of ten he was teaching India's pundits about the *Vedas* which he had never read, interpreting abstruse passages and pointing out errors. He claims to be omnipresent, omniscient, and omnipotent. He once made the amazing statement that he could if he wished bring the universe to an end.

He began his mission at the age of thirteen, with an ashram about the size of a tin hut. Today the ashram is about two acres in extent, with accommodation for 10,000 visitors, and a prayer hall (the poornachandra) which is the biggest in Asia. Puttaparthi is rapidly becoming the Vatican of the East.

He claims 50 million devotees in the world, with centres

61

in over 60 countries outside India. He is certainly the most potent force, both spiritually and in the secular field, in the whole of the Indian continent. On a whirlwind trip to Delhi, tens of thousands of humble folk await his *darshan* (blessing) and India's leading figures (the president, the ex-prime minister, foreign ambassadors, professors at universities) seek his counsel. Many believe that in a decade or two's time he will be the most potent force in the world. His mission is to save the world from a nuclear holocaust. He has said: 'The catastrophe which has come to mankind will be averted. A new Golden Age will recur. I shall not fail, it is not in the nature of avatars to fail.'

His recorded miracles number tens of thousands, his unrecorded miracles probably millions. He heals the sick, controls the elements, materializes anything he wishes from nothing, has raised the dead on two occasions.

There is no question about his validity. Dr Bhagavantam, India's leading nuclear physicist, has said, 'For the past fifteen years I have witnessed Sai Baba materialize an infinite number of objects at will. He has cured virtually every disease known to man. I have, therefore, to declare this man a Transcendental Being, Divine.' Dr Gokak, another close aide, has written: 'No previous avatar has been attested to by such an army of professional people.' He has been examined by scientists, philosophers, psychic researchers the world over.

The advent of this Master has been prophesied in the world's scriptures. There is a reference in the nineteenth chapter of *St John's Revelations*. The *Upanishads* refer to it 5,600 years ago. There are palm-leaf manuscripts intact in India by the sage, Shuka, who prophesied his name and the exact date and place of his birth and, perhaps most remarkable of all, in the thirteenth chapter of the *Ocean of Light*, a collation of the sayings of Mahomet, there are three hundred details which exactly fit Sai Baba, including such mundane details as a bridge on his nose, a gap in his teeth, and a mole on his left cheek!

Sai Baba teaches the universality of all faiths (his emblem which is sculptured on all his buildings being the symbols of the five major religions). The cornerstone of his teachings is the brotherhood of man through the common inheritance of the *atma* (divine spark), and that God is Love, that Love is the fundamental law of the Cosmos. This latter may seem like a cliché to some but in the divine discourses of the avatar and the way he manifests love in his daily life, a new insight and a new reality is given to the word. Sai Baba is indeed the embodiment of Love.

Who then is this world phenomenon? I will quote from a statement he made at the first world conference in Bombay in 1968 which he has repeated many times: 'In this human form of Sai every Divine Principle, every Divine Entity, that is to say all the names and forms which man has ascribed for God, are manifest.'

It is hard to believe but after the incomparable blessing of seven interviews, in inspired moments, I have come to believe just this. As he says: 'Call me by any name, Krishna, Allah, Christ . . . can you not recognize me in any form?'

Ron Laing, MA (Cantab).
Member Sathya Sai World Council.

Sathya Sai Baba The Embodiment of Love by Peggy Mason and Ron Laing, MA.

£3.90 + postage (postage at time of writing is 75p). Available from the Psychic News Bookshop, 20 Earlham Street, London WC2, or your local bookshop.

Single signed copies from the authors, The Lodge, 10 Broadwater Down, Tunbridge Wells, Kent. *Sathya Sai Baba The Embodiment of Love*, is published by Sawbridge Enterprises, 37 Sydney Street, London SW3.

The following profile is in the form of an official 'release' and it is worth reading both accounts because there are items of information and insights which are contained in the one profile but not in the other. I feel that both 'impressions' give an excellent projection of Sai Baba, and they should prompt interested readers to obtain any one of the many Sai Baba books which are available, some of which are mentioned in this chapter.

At the end of this chapter, you will find a listing of Sri Sathya Sai Centres, Bhajan Centres and groups within the United Kingdom.

Brief Information About Bhagavan Shri Sathya Sai Baba

Shri Sathya Sai Baba was born on 23 November 1926 at Puttaparthi, a tiny remote village in South India. He was named Sathyanarayana but called Sathya by the family and villages. At the time of this birth many favourable omens were seen in the house. Even as a boy of seven, he composed hymns and wrote scripts and songs for religious dramas and morality plays. He materialized or produced from the air, by a mere wave of his palm, objects like fruit, flowers and sweets for his comrades. When he was fourteen years of age, his divine powers came into bloom. He could transcend the dimensions of space and time to bless the seekers and sufferers even in far-off places. Baba's name spread far and wide as the Divine Boy of Puttaparthi. At this time Baba declared his mission and left home saying, 'I am going. My people are calling me. My task is to reorganize society and revive the good life through the awareness of the divinity of man.' He announced that he was Sathya Sai Baba – Sathya (Truth), Sai (Holy Mother), Baba (Father). 'Come to me with empty hands,' says Baba, 'so that I can fill them with joy and peace.'

Sai Baba has performed innumerable and unbelievable miracles such as the healing of incurable diseases like cancer and paralysis and the raising of the dead. There are hundreds and thousands of people/devotees who have regained their eyesight, speech and hearing. Many crippled and handicapped sufferers have been miraculously healed, and many of them are still living and enjoying the reward of their devotion and his grace.

Baba says, 'God is present where his glory is sung,' and in many devotees' homes all over the world, Baba shows his presence by appearing as sacred ash (*vibhuti*) or red powder (*kum kum*) or ambrosia (*amrit*) or a flow of honey on photographs of his present form or any pictures of Jesus, Buddha, Siva and Rama.

Every morning and evening Baba gives his *darshan* (audience) to the vast crowd which gathers outside his residence. Baba selects deserving souls for interviews and discloses to them their innermost life secrets. He tells about past, present and future life and grants boons, proving that he knows all about us.

Baba produces in a few seconds, by a wave of his right hand in circular movements, any object in gold or silver or any fruit (even out of season) or item of food or articles which are available only in faraway lands, to fulfil the wishes of his devotees.

The Sathya Sai message is simple, sweet and sustaining and above all it is loving and universal in outlook and appeal. Therefore, there are more than 3,000 units of the Sathya Sai Seva Organization in all the continents, from New Zealand to Iceland, from Trinidad to Thailand. They are engaged in implementing the message in their lives, social relations and spiritual exercises. Baba's followers are counted in millions. They profess loyalty to different religions and their loyalty is reinforced by faith in Baba's message of love and service. They include eminent scholars and writers, thinkers and technocrats, scientists and administrators, judges and jurists, doctors and psychiatrists, industrialists and poets. Baba assures them, 'I have not come to destroy or disturb your faith or vocation. I desire to confirm your faith and sublimate your desires. I have come to make everyone realize the one God within

65

each, to urge everyone to live in peace, harmony and love and to prompt everyone to strive for the happiness of one another. I have come to reconstruct the ancient highway to God. My task is the spiritual regeneration of humanity through truth and love. This Sai has come in order to achieve the supreme task of uniting as one family entire mankind through the bond of brotherhood, of affirming and illumining the atomic reality of each being in order to reveal the Divine which is the basis on which the entire cosmos rests.'

In respect of the surprisingly diverse, difficult and miraculous things which he accomplishes, he gives a simple answer: 'There is no mesmerism, miracle or magic in what I do! Mine is genuine divine power. I am the indweller of every heart.' It is indeed difficult, if not impossible, for any human being to comprehend, analyse and understand him. He says, 'My life is my message,' and with this declaration he exhorts us to be exemplary men and women.

Baba gives the following explanation as to why the Lord has to incarnate: 'For the protection of the virtuous, for the destruction of evildoers and for establishing righteousness on a firm footing. Whenever disharmony overwhelms the world, the Lord will incarnate in human form to establish the modes of earning peace and to re-educate the human community in the paths of peace.'

Devotees of all religions go to him with great faith and are benefited. He says, 'There is no need to change your chosen God and adopt a new one when you have seen me and heard me. Continue your worship of your chosen God along the lines already familiar to you, then you will find that you are coming nearer and nearer to me; for all names are mine and all forms are mine.'

Baba says:

> There is only race – the race of humanity
> There is only one language – the language of the heart
> There is only one religion – the religion of love
> There is only one God – God, the omnipresent.

Prasanthi Nilayam or the Abode of Perfect Peace (in Puttaparthi) has now become an international spiritual centre. Thousands in quest of light and love proceed to that place to be inspired by Baba and guided by him. Wherever Baba is – Brindavan near Bangalore, Prasanthi Nilayam in Anantpur District, Dharmakshetra in Bombay, and Delhi – Baba finds himself surrounded by thousands of aspirants eager to secure a glimpse of the avatar (incarnation) of the age and hear a few words of his divine message.

At each of the 3,000 plus centres working all over the world under his guidance, Baba's message of truth, justice, peace and love is heard by hundreds of sincere men and women. Service to the handicapped and the downtrodden, regular sessions of meditation, congregational prayers, study circles intent on spiritual texts of all kinds and creeds and moral education of children are the programmes undertaken in each centre.

In short, Shri Sathya Sai Service (Seva) Organization's main plank of activity is, as Baba directs, 'Serve man – serve God.' This, Baba says, is the way to the Kingdom of God within man, by which mankind can realize the fatherhood of God and the brotherhood of man.

The Sai Ram Centre

Grateful thanks are given to Mr R Kapur of the Sai Ram Centre, who not only supplied me with the *Brief Information About Bhagavan Shri Sathya Sai Baba* but who also enlightened me further on the subject of Sai Baba.

The Sai Ram Centre was established in London during October 1979 with the blessing of Sai Baba in order to spread his divine message to all. This is done through the media of films, books, photographs and cassettes of devotional songs. The Centre also has in stock 8mm and 16mm films viz: 1) *Advent of the Avatar*; 2) *Shri Sathya Sai Baba – North India Tour, Spring 1973*; 3) *Darshan – A Vision of Reality*; 4) *Divine Presence*; 5) *Sai Baba The Early Years*; 6) *The Lost Years of Jesus*, covering the missing eighteen years in the life of Jesus. These films are shown at the Centre or they can be made available to be shown elsewhere. Currently in stock are two films on video cassettes, which can be bought for use on home television sets.

The Sai Ram Centre is a mine of information on Sai Baba and samples of healing ash (*vibhuti*) can be obtained there. The Centre is conveniently located, literally around the corner from Swiss Cottage Underground Station.

Address: Sai Ram Centre, 1 Harben Parade, Finchley Road, London NW3.
Tel. (01) 586 7117; (01) 586 7118

Sri Sathya Sai Centres and Study Circles in the UK
Sri Sathya Sai Centres (Educational, Philosophical and Welfare Centres)

London

Central

Sri Sathya Sai Seva Organization* Central London (Mr Puri)
   39, Sudbury Court Drive, Harrow, Middlesex. Tel: (01) 904 8755

South

Sri Sathya Sai Centre (South London) (Dr Nath)
   Abbotswood, Bridle Way, Addington, Croydon, Surrey. Tel: (01) 777 0464

East

Sri Sathya Sai Centre (Ilford) (Mr Tandon)
   16 Worcester Garden, Ilford, Essex. Tel: (01) 554 1592

West

Sri Sathya Sai Centre – West (Hounslow) (Mr Tankaria)
   30 Haslemere Avenue, Hounslow West, Middlesex. Tel: (01) 759 2994

South-West

Sri Sathya Sai Baba Centre of Graveney (Mr Victor Kanu)
   Devereux House, 50 Longley Road, London SW17. Tel: (01) 672 9570
Sri Sathya Sai Centre – Tooting (Mr Kiritbhai Patel)
      * Service to the community and welfare work.

69

66 Ashvale Road, Tooting Broadway, London SW17.
Tel: (01) 672 6231

South East
Sri Sathya Sai Centre (Mr Raman Solanki)
45 Broxholm Road, West Norwood, London SW27. Tel:
(01) 761 1602

Outer London
Sri Sathya Sai Centre (Mr S Talwar)
5 Meadow Road, Southall, Middlesex. Tel: (01) 571
1647
Sri Sathya Sai Centre (Mr Manubhai Patel)
35 Clifton Avenue, Wembley, Middlesex. Tel: (01) 903
0886

Birmingham

Sri Sathya Sai Centre (Mr Narsibhai Patel)
81 Beach Road, Spark Hill, Birmingham 11. Tel: (021)
773 3638
Sri Sathya Sai Centre (Mr Popatbhai Parmar)
215 Bankes Road, Small Heath, Birmingham 10. Tel:
(021) 772 2824
Sri Sathya Sai Centre (Mr Ravjibhai Patel)
110 Esme Road, Sparkhill, Birmingham 11. Tel: (021)
449 8011
Sri Sathya Sai Centre (Dr M R Patel)
44 Woodend, Handsworth Wood, Birmingham 20. Tel:
(021) 357 8173

Bolton

Sri Sathya Sai Centre (Mr Vinubhai Patel)
95 Eldon Street, Bolton 2, Lancashire. Tel: (0204) 35298

Bradford

Sri Sathya Sai Centre (Mr Gulabbhai Patel)
10 Laisteridge Lane, Great Horton Road, Bradford 7,
West Yorkshire. Tel: (0274) 28530

Coventry

Sri Sathya Sai Centre (Mrs Shantaben S Patel)
15 Parkville Way, Holbrooke, Coventry. Tel: (0203) 84269

Sri Sathya Sai Centre (Mr Rameshbhai Patel)
9 Cambridge Street, Hillfields, Coventry. Tel: (0203) 29331

Glasgow

Sri Sathya Sai Centre (Dr C L Anand)
34 Vorlich Gardens, Bearsden, Glasgow. Tel: (041) 943 1440

Hatfield

Sri Sathya Sai Centre (Mr Amrithanandan)
62 Herns Lane, Welwyn Garden City, Hertfordshire. Tel: (07073) 26314

Leicester

Sri Sathya Sai Centre (Mr Navinbhai Patel)
18 Coles Close, Leicester 4, Leicestershire. Tel: (0533) 66902

Loughborough

Sri Sathya Sai Centre (Mr Dayaljibhai Patel)
15 Albert Promenade, Loughborough, Leicestershire. Tel: (0509) 218233

Manchester

Sri Sathya Sai Centre (Mr Morarbhai Patel)
27 Turnbull Road, Longsight, Manchester 13. Tel: (061) 224 5369

Nuneaton

Sri Sathya Sai Centre (Mr Bhikhubhai Patel)
36 Norman Avenue, Nuneaton, Warwickshire. Tel: (0203) 643713

Walsall
Sri Sathya Sai Centre (Mr Rameshbhai A Patel)
24 Arundel Street, Calmor Area, Walsall 1. Tel: (0922)
612982

Wellingborough
Sri Sathya Sai Centre (Mr Gulabbhia Bharati)
2 Grant Road, Wellingborough, Northants. Tel: (0933)
224124

Wolverhampton
Sri Sathya Sai Centre (Mr Ratilal Patel)
30 Lonsdale Road, Pennfields, Wolverhampton, Staffordshire. Tel: (0902) 331668.

Sri Sathya Sai Bhajan Centres in UK (Devotional Groups – Worship and Singing)

London
North
Sri Sathya Sai Bhajan Centre (Mr Charanjit Manchanda)
184 Stapleton Hall Road, London N4. Tel: (01) 348
0285
Sri Sathya Sai Bhajan Centre (Mrs K Ganesh)
60 Eade Road, London N4. Tel: (01) 800 4103

North West

Sri Sathya Sai Bhajan Centre (Mr Nand Kishore)
Sai Villa, 56 Bridge Lane, London NW11. Tel: (01) 458 8207

Sri Sathya Sai Bhajan Centre (Mr Sharaf)
9 Fairfield Crescent, Kingsbury NW9. Tel: (01) 204 7582

East

Sri Sathya Sai Bhajan Centre (Mr Pinkraj)
614 Romford Road, Manor Park, London E12. Tel: (01) 478 6066

Sri Sathya Sai Bhajan Centre (Mr Juneja)
81 Second Avenue, London E12. Tl: (01) 514 3905

Sri Sathya Sai Bhajan Centre (Mrs Geetaben, c/o Geeta Art)
261 Green Street, Forest Gate, London E7. Tel: (01) 552 4873

West

Sri Sathya Sai Bhajan Centre (R Saggar)
39 North Field Avenue, West Ealing, London W3. Tel: (01) 576 5235

South West

Sri Sathya Sai Bhajan Centre (Mr R Sivayogan)
127 Effra Road, London SW19. Tel: (01) 460 2563
(Alternative contact address: 8 Oakham Drive, Bromley, Kent)

Outer London

Sri Sathya Sai Bhajan Centre (Mrs Chuthani)
127 Cowley Hill, Borehamwood, Hertfordshire. Tel: (01) 953 2477

Sri Sathya Sai Bhajan Centre (Mr S V Deo)
25 Montague Road, Hendon, London NW4. Tel: (01) 202 8067

Sri Sathya Sai Bhajan Centre (Mr Chadha)
434 Staines Road, Hounslow Heath Post Office, Hounslow. Tel: (01) 572 7546

Sri Sathya Sai Bhajan Centre (Mr M R Kundra)
 21–23 Richmond Road, Ilford, Essex. Tel: (01) 478 4107
Sri Sathya Sai Bhajan Centre (Mr C Nathwani)
 33 Kingshill Avenue, Kenton. Tel: (01) 907 6201
Sri Sathya Sai Bhajan Centre (Mr Malhotra)
 11 Lulworth Close, Rayners Lane, Harrow. Tel: (01)
 422 3596
Sri Sathya Sai Bhajan Centre (Mr B Arora)
 24a Lady Margret Road, Southall, Middlesex. Tel: (01)
 571 2346
Sri Sathya Sai Bhajan Centre (Mr Anoop Shah)
 116 Fairland Avenue, Thornton Heath, Surrey. Tel:
 (01) 684 5016

Birmingham
Sri Sathya Sai Bhajan Centre (Mr Narayan Rao)
 27 Masters Lane, Halesowen, Birmingham. Tel: (021)
 559 3142

Blackpool
Sri Sathya Sai Bhajan Centre (Mr Ajit Patnaik)
 152 Norbreck Road, Blackpool. Tel: (0253) 826007

Bradford
Sri Sathya Sai Bhajan Centre (Mr Dayabhai Patel)
 15 Fairbank Road, Bradford 8.
Sri Sathya Sai Bhajan Centre (Mr Bhikhubhai Patel)
 45 Weetwood Road, Bradford.
Sri Sathya Sai Bhajan Centre (Mr Mohanbhai Patel)
 432 Great Horton Road, Bradford 7. Tel: (0274) 577106
Sri Sathya Sai Bhajan Centre (Mr Naranbhai Patel)
 17 Rand Street, Bradford 7.
Sri Sathya Sai Bhajan Centre (Mr Maheshbhai Patel)
 53 Horton Grange Road, Bradford 7.
Sri Sathya Sai Bhajan Centre (Mr Purushottam Mistry)
 162 Horton Grange Road, Bradford 7.

Cardiff

Sri Sathya Sai Bhajan Centre (Mrs S P Patel)
118 Mardy Street, Grangtown, Cardiff. Tel: (0222)
35211

Coventry

Sri Sathya Sai Bhajan Centre (Mr Rameshbhai Patel)
9 Cambridge Street, Hillfields, Coventry. Tel: (0233)
29331

Gunnislake

Sri Sathya Sai Bhajan Centre (Mr Harry Manbridge)
13 St Elmo, Bealswood Road, Gunnislake, Cornwall.

Huddersfield

Sri Sathya Sai Bhajan Centre (Mr Gurudutt Bali)
34 Hawthorn Terrace, Huddersfield, West Yorkshire.
Tel: (0484) 511456

Leeds

Sri Sathya Sai Bhajan Centre (Mr Ranchhodbhai Patel)
125 Upper Wortley Road, Leeds 12, West Yorkshire.
Tel: (0532) 638801

Leicester

Sri Sathya Sai Bhajan Centre (Mr Balubhai Mistry)
72 Bonsall Street, Leicester. Tel: (0533) 543109
Sri Sathya Sai Bhajan Centre (Mrs Shantaben G Patel)
189 Trevino Drive, Rushey Mead, Leicester. Tel: (0533)
65271

Northwood

Sri Sathya Sai Bhajan Centre (Mr Sarin)
27 Bennett Close, off Chester Road, Northwood, Middlesex. Tel: (09274) 29768

Nottingham
Sri Sathya Sai Bhajan Centre (Mrs Vimala Shetty)
52 Balmoral Drive, Bramcote Hills, Beeston, Nottingham, Nottinghamshire. Tel: (0602) 258333

Oldham
Sri Sathya Sai Bhajan Centre (Mr Bharat Sisodiya)
53 Cornish Way, Royton, Oldham, Lancashire. Tel: (0706) 844994

Rugby
Sri Sathya Sai Bhajan Centre (Mr N Mistry)
29 Manor Road, Rugby, Warwickshire. Tel: (0788) 70910/70912

Salisbury
Sri Sathya Sai Bhajan Centre (Mrs James Furguson)
6 Folkestone Road, Salisbury, Wilts.

Slough
Sri Sathya Sai Bhajan Centre (Mr H Chaudhary)
22 Whitby Road, Slough, Buckinghamshire.

Sri Sathya Sai Study Circles in UK
(Study of Sai Baba's Teachings)

London
Sri Sathya Sai Study Circle (Mr Sita Ram)
Om Sai, 19 The Chequers, West End Lane, Pinner. Tel: (01) 866 6496

Isle of Wight
Sri Sathya Sai Study Circle (Mr Ron Miller)
24 St Johns Road, Newport, Isle of Wight. Tel: (0983)
522447

Norfolk
Bhajan Group and Study Circle (Mrs Kit Robinson)
  2 Simpson Close, North Walsham, Norfolk.

Portadown
Sri Sathya Sai Study Circle (Mr Satya Paul)
  71 Kingsway Drive, Portadown, Northern Ireland. Tel:
  (0762) 35013

Sheffield
Sri Sathya Sai Study Circle (Mr A Robinson)
  22 Gardom Close, Dronfield Wood House, Sheffield.
  Tel: (0246) 416224

Sutton-in-Craven
Sri Sathya Sai Study Circle (Mr Bernard Movay)
  43 Main Street, Sutton-in Craven, West Yorkshire.
  Telephone enquiries to Mr Gulabbhai Patel, Bradford.
  Tel: (0274) 28530

Tunbridge Wells
UK Representative on the Sathya Sai World Council, Mr
Ron Laing
  The Lodge, 10 Broadwater Down, Tunbridge Wells,
  Kent. Tel: (0892) 21592

Directory of Mediums, Psychics and Astrologers

London

AUGUSTUS, John: Clairvoyance, numerology, astrology, Tarot, crystal and colour/meditation healing. Private and postal readings plus travel. International psychic consultant and specialist in 'life direction'.

Address: Flat A, 10 Edgarley Terrace, Fulham, London SW6.
Tel: (01) 731 2236

BAIZLEY, G: Welsh African seer. Clairvoyance and clairaudience. This medium has inherited Celtic and West African psychic gifts from his parents. Private readings.

Address: 44 Elam Close, Minet Road, London SE5.
Tel: (01) 733 1816

BARHAM, Irene: Clairvoyance and clairaudience. Also healing. Private and postal readings. She will travel and attends groups and churches.

Address: 26 Robinson Road, Tooting, London SW17.
Tel: (01) 540 4365

BASHIR, Mir: Hand analyst, author and lecturer. Personal and postal consultations. Over the past forty years, Mir Bashir has addressed a great variety of audiences throughout Asia, Africa and the United States of America and the United Kingdom. He has had extensive media coverage and, apart from private consultations, he has given lectures and seminars on the Art of Hand Analysis.

Address: 839 Finchley Road, London NW11.
Tel: (01) 458 4321/4322

BOURNE, Brian: BAPS consultant, NFSH and membership of the Society of Psychic Research. Tarot, sand and auragraphs. Brian Bourne is also a psychotherapist and hypnotherapist. Private consultations and postal Tarot readings. He will travel and appears professionally at psychic festivals. Apart from divination, healing and festival work, he has had about fifteen years' experience dealing with negative psychic phenomena such as hauntings, poltergeist activity and exorcisms.

Address: 36 Osney House, Thamesmead Estate, London SE2.
Tel: (01) 311 3449

BRACE, Louise: Clairvoyance. Also spiritual guidance and healing. Private readings and occasional travel.

Address: 203 Kyverdale Road, Stamford Hill, London N16.

BRADY, Julia: Psychic consultant, healer and lecturer. Clairvoyance, clairaudience, astrology and Tarot. Private and postal consultations plus travel.

Address: 7 Jago Close, Plumstead, London SE18.
Tel: (01) 317 9210

BROUGH-ELEY, Leslie, GWRM: Clairvoyance, clairaudience and healing. Private consultations and travel. This medium is also a healer who lists relaxation techniques and massage as methods used. Churches served.

Address: First Floor Flat, 28 Craven Terrace, Lancaster Gate, London W2.
Tel: (01) 723 2781

CAROLE and NORMAN: Astrology, Tarot and runes (Anglo-Saxon tradition). Private consultations only. Carole and Norman also run courses on astrology, Tarot and meditation, all of which are aligned with ancient Egyptian teaching. The Egyptian Esoteric Society is also run by these two psychics.

Address: 43 Bennett House, Page Street, London SW1.
Tel: (01) 821 0237

COLLINS, Ziata: Cairvoyance, clairaudience, psychometry and cartomancy. This medium may use one or a combination of divining systems, depending on the circumstances at the time. Private consultations are by appointment. Clairvoyance has run in this medium's family for over 200 years and Ziata has great respect for her inherited psychic gifts.

Tel: (01) 267 9580

DABROWA, Betty: Clairvoyance and absent healing. Postal readings only.

Address: 21 Paston Close, Millfields Estate, Millfields Road, Clapton, London E5.
Tel: (01) 986 1777

DAVIES, Fredrick: Psychic astrologer. Studied astrology at the institute of the Hollywood-based Carroll Righter, reputedly Ronald Reagan's astrologer. He also studied psychic arts under the Apache and Mexican Indians. Astrology, clairvoyance, numerology and Tarot. Fredrick Davies has had extensive media coverage here and in the United States of America. He was resident astrologer on the BBC2 TV series *Star Signs*. He predicts for *Horoscopes* in *Vogue* magazine and commutes between London and New York. He can be contacted via his London office. Clients are seen in the West End.

Addresses: 36 Clyde Road, Wood Green, London N22.
Tel: (01) 888 7295;

30 Lincoln Plaza, New York, NY 10023, USA.
Tel: (0101) 212 755 6110

DOUGAL, Alan: Clairvoyance and clairaudience. Private and postal readings plus travel.

Address: 21 Sandford Avenue, Wood Green, London N22.
Tel: (01) 889 0719

DURNIN, Jackie: Astrology and Tarot. Also dream interpretation, healing and counselling – counselling for emotional tension and depression, using natural flower remedies. Postal consultation only.

Address: 35 Embassy House, West End Lane, London NW6.

ELLIS, Dawn: Clairvoyance and the ancient art of cartomancy. Private consultations and travel within London. Dawn will give psychic advice on all problems.

Address: 1037 Finchley Road, Temple Fortune, London NW11.
Tel: (01) 458 9993

EVERETT, Lee: The House of Spirit. Clairvoyance, clairaudience, clearances, healing, meditation and regression. Private consultations and travel. The House of Spirit is a house of healing and the development of the human being through self-knowledge and meditation. Lee Everett's autobiography *The Happy Medium* was published in 1983 by MacDonald Futura.

Address: 30 Artesian Road, London W2.
Tel: (01) 727 9175

GAINEY: Clairvoyance, astrology and healing. Gainey gives private and postal readings and also travels.

Address: 99 Sir Oswald Stoll Mansions, Fulham Road, London SW6.
Tel: (01) 785 0411

GARMAN, Joan: Clairvoyance and clairaudience. Private and postal readings. Postal readings can be given from photographs which are returnable. She is also a healer.

Address: BCM/Daffodils, London WC1.
Tel: (01) 680 2851

GHANI, M A: Astrology, numerology and healing. Private and postal readings. Practitioner of *Ill-Me-Jaffer*, the science of ancient Arabian numerology. Specializes in spiritual cures for hypertension, infertility and barrenness in women. Astrological consultant. Prepares talismans from the Koran scriptures.

Address: 155 Upper Tooting Road, London SW17.
Tel: (01) 767 6058

GRADWELL, Henry Stephen: Tarot. Postal only. A booklet has been published to help enquirers understand the Tarot.

Address: 386 Lea Bridge Road, Leyton, London E10.

HARLEQUIN, The: Tarot card clairvoyant. Private and postal (via tape) readings. Also travel. Clairvoyance, clairaudience, astrology, numerology, Tarot and crystal. Long-standing knowledge and experience of the occult and spiritual worlds, plus all kindred matters, eg: dream interpretations. Healing also given. Guidance and help concerning personal and intimate problems, both spiritual and mundane.

Address: 56 Bowmans Buildings, Penfold Place, London NW1.
Tel: (01) 724 0765

HOWARTH, Sybil: Clairvoyance, numerology, Tarot, crystal.

Address: BCM/Camomile, Monomark House, London WC1.

INGMAR, Madam: I-Ching. Private and postal readings. She is a graduate Sinologist who has lived and worked in China.

Address: 80 Wakeman Road, London NW10.
Tel: (01) 969 1171 ~~wrong no.~~

JACKSON, Wendy: Clairvoyance, clairaudience, numerology, palmistry and Tarot. Also healing and herbalism. Private consultations and travel. Wendy Jackson also runs the Pegasus teaching group. Enquirers are invited to telephone for details of meetings.

Address: 2 York Road, Upper Edmonton, London N18.
Tel: (01) 807 6383

JAMES: Astrology (Kabbalistic Astrology) and Tarot. Private and postal consultations. James is the author of seven books; three of them on the subject of the Kabbala, one on gemstones, one on aromatics, one on vibrations and one on twelve rays. He is the editor of the quarterly magazine *The Kabbalist*, and co-principal of the International Order of Kabbalists.

Address: 25 Circle Gardens, Merton Park, London SW19.
Tel: (01) 542 3611

KAZ: Tarot, astrology, numerology, runes, crystal and I-Ching. Kaz says that her use of the above 'working tools' is 'based on a wide, perhaps idealistic field of application. I am not, therefore, particularly concerned with the problems of health, wealth and success in the more usual run-of-the-mill sense, although I do give readings (by appointment only) where, in at least some way, however small, this will help the subject to better understand themselves.'

Address: Kaz BM, Kaz RE-AL, London WC1.

LARNO, A: Clairvoyance, crystal and palmistry. Private and postal readings. All postal enquiries must be accompanied by a stamped and self-addressed envelope. Telephone enquiries should be made before 6 pm.

Address: 118 Gordon Road, Ealing, London W13.
Tel: (01) 997 4113

LAWRENCE, Dr Richard H, BAPS: Clairvoyance, clairaudience and crystal. This psychic consultant will give private readings by appointment.

Address: The Aetherius Society, 757 Fulham Road, London SW6.
Tel: (01) 736 4187/731 1094

LENA: Clairvoyance, clairaudience and Tarot. Private consultations only. Healing is given if requested.

Address: 15 Landward Court, Harrowby Street, London W1.
Tel: (01) 402 2906

LESTER, Aislinn: Clairvoyance, clairaudience, I-Ching, numerology, Tarot, crystal, psychometry and private Tarot tuition for suitable applicants. A certificate is available on completion of the course. She is also a healer who gives contact and absent healing. Her speciality is colour healing and private tuition is available for auric reading in conjunction with colour healing. A certificate is available on completion of the course.

Address: Phoenix Lodge, 1 Lysia Street, Fulham, London SW6.
Tel: (01) 385 5637

LUXON, Bettina: Clairvoyance, Tarot and palmistry. Private and postal consultations. Bettina has formed a penpal club for senior citizens and has to date received 2,000 letters in response to her weekly magazine.

Address: 24 Atheneaum Court, Highbury New Park, London N5.
Tel. (01) 454 2646.

MAMDANI, Salim, FOS MICH: This psychic is also a consultant palmist, numerologist, graphologist, chiro-psychologist, hypnotist, healer and a consultant for the British Astrological/Psychic Society. Private consultations are by appointment only. Salim Mamdani was born of Indian parents in Dar es Salaam, Tanzania. He is the seventh son of a seventh son and such people are usually well-endowed with mystic and occult gifts. Salim Mamdani has featured in several *TV Times* articles.

Address: 88a Isledon Road, London N7.
Tel: (01) 609 0419

MURIEL: Clairvoyance, clairaudience and healing. Private consultations for ladies only. This Wimbledon-based medium is also a healer.

Tel. (01) 946 1566

PANDYA, Ashwin: Clairvoyance, palmistry, numerology, phrenology, remedial massage therapy and reflexology. Telephone or write to enquire about private appointments.

Address: 65b Aberdare Gardens, London NW6.
Tel: (01) 328 6091

PARSONS, Robert A, GWRM: Clairvoyance, clairaudience and cartomancy. Private readings, churches served, and travel including travel abroad. Fluent in French.

Tel: (01) 352 6519

PEARSE, Lilian: Clairvoyance and clairaudience. Medium, spiritual healer and exorcist. Private appointments only. She will travel any distance to perform exorcisms or remove evil influences. She also specializes in treating nervous and emotional conditions.

Address: Silver Cross Healing Sanctuary, 19a Coldershaw Road, West Ealing, London W13.
Tel: (01) 579 1039

PEPLOW, Mrs Patricia: Palmistry and Tarot. Also healing, masseuse, Chinese acupressure. Private and postal consultations plus travel. This psychic recently completed a one-month trip to Singapore and Malaysia. Word of mouth recommendation kept her appointment book full until she returned to England.

Address: 36 Elliott Road, Chiswick, London W4.
Tel: (01) 994 2654

PLAYER, Kathryn: Clairvoyance and Tarot. Also private and absent healing.

Address: Box BCM Sapphire, British Monomarks, Old Gloucester Road, London WC1.
Tel: (01) 690 3824 (message service number for use between 6–8pm)

POTTS, Owen: Clairvoyance, clairaudience, Tarot, hypnotherapy, trance and healing. Private and telephone consultations.

Address: 4 Abingdon Close, Wimbledon, London SW19.
Tel: (01) 540 2779

POTTS, Sue: Clairvoyance, astrology and Tarot. Private and postal readings. Local travel only. Also takes classes for astrology and Tarot plus psychic development.

Address: 4 Abingdon Close, Wimbledon, London SW19.
Tel: (01) 540 2779

RAE, Margaret, SNU ISM BAPS (Consultant): Clairvoyance, clairaudience, healing, musical medium. Psychic consultant/adviser in psychotherapy with experience in the Samaritans. She gives private and postal readings and also travels.

Address: 120 Campden Houses, Peel Street, London W8.
Tel: (01) 727 0800

RACHAEL, Jane: Astrology and Tarot. Private readings plus lectures and workshops. Some interesting media coverage in relation to her particular approach to divination.

Address: 41 Mornington Crescent, London NW1.
Tel: (01) 734 3356 ~~wrong no~~

SARENNE Kensington-based Tarot card reader. Private readings that last from two to four hours.

Tel: (01) 221 7888 or (01) 937 9801

SCOTT, Harry H: Contact and absent healing from a sanctuary.

Address: 338 Wickham Lane, London SE2.
Tel: (01) 732 8481

SINGH, Krishna P, MA BSc LT: Spiritual help through talismans/occult. Postal only or special personal consultations.

Address: 79 Carlyle Road, Manor Park, London E12.

STAVES, Marjorie: Clairvoyance. Write or telephone to enquire about readings.

Address: 3 Crofton House, 1 New Cavendish Street, London W1.
Tel: (01) 487 3675

TERRY: Clairvoyance, clairaudience, numerology and Tarot. The main emphasis of his work is on clairvoyance and clairaudience. Private and postal readings and some travel.

Address: 60 Devon Mansions, Tooley Street, London SE1.
Also: 40 Tunley Road, Upper Tooting, London SW17.
Tel: (01) 407 9147/673 7656

THEODORA, Madame: Clairvoyance, crystal and magic mirror. Telephone appointments for genuine enquirers only. Private readings.

Tel: (01) 834 5696

UBELS, Edward, BTS BAPS CPS: Tarot and clairaudience. Private readings.

Address: 7 Prebend Mansions, Chiswick High Road, London W4.
Tel: (01) 994 3564

WOOD, Glorie: I-Ching. Private and postal readings.

Address: 146 Finchley Road, London NW3.
Tel: (01) 794 2941

YASMINE: West London-based medium. Clairvoyance, clairaudience, Tarot and I-Ching. Private consultations and travel with occasional attendance for functions. Telephone to make appointments.

Tel: (01) 221 0049

Birmingham

STARKEY, John: Clairvoyance and clairaudience. Also travel. In addition, he specializes in enquiries, investigations, special interest weekends and psychic exhibitions.

Address: 7a Newton Road, Great Barr, Birmingham 43.
Tel: (021) 358 1409 or (0922) 648109

Glasgow

WILSON, Carole E, DF Astrol S: Astrology. Shawlands, Glasgow-based astrologer who gives private and postal readings. Telephone consultations can also be given if travel is a problem for clients.

Tel: 041-632 3661

Liverpool

STARR, Liliane Mitchell: Clairvoyance, clairaudience, psychometry and healing. Private and postal consultations plus travel.

Address: 16a Parkfield Road, Aigberth, Liverpool 17.
Tel: (051) 728 7076

WARICK, J: Numerology, astrology and cartomancy (standard playing cards). Private and postal readings. No callers, please – readings by prior postal arrangement only.

Address: 17 Watergate Lane, Woolton, Liverpool 25.

Manchester

ROEBUCK, Charles W: Astrology, hororay astrology and Tarot. Private and postal consultations. Postal readings are on cassettes.

Address: 10 Cromer Avenue, Denton, Manchester 34.
Tel: (061) 320 8065

Avon

ANDERSON, Keith: Palmistry and alternative medicine selected by dowsing. Private and postal readings.

Address: 21 Carnarvon Road, Redland, Bristol.

HARPER, John, DMS Astrol BAPS: Consultant. Astrology. Private and postal readings. He will travel within the

Bristol area. This astrologer is also a consultant for the Mayo School of Astrology.

Address: 4 Drayton Close, Whitchurch Park, Bristol 14.
Tel: (0272) 830952

ACUSHLA: Tarot and palmistry. Private and postal readings. Acushla's consultation hours are between 10am and 4.30pm, Tuesday to Saturday. Her consultation suite is centrally located near the famous Bath Pump Room.

Address: 21 Stall Street, Bath, Avon.
Tel: (02214) 68720 (telephone during evenings)

Bedfordshire

CEPHAS, Peter: Clairvoyance, psychometry and healing. Private and postal readings plus travel for any spiritual work. No charge is made but donations are accepted.

Address: 81 Reginald Street, Luton, Bedfordshire.
Tel: (0582) 423928

JEHANE: Cartomancy. Private and postal readings plus party bookings. She uses standard playing cards for divination.

Address: 132 Hart Lane, Luton, Bedfordshire.
Tel: (0582) 21345

Berkshire

YOUNG, Millicent M C: Clairvoyance, clairaudience and numerology. Private and postal readings. Mrs Young has been a practising medium for thirteen years and speaks regularly at the Reading National Spiritualist Church, 81 Baker Street.

Address: 32 Haddon Drive, Woodley, Near Reading, Berkshire.
Tel: (0734) 695561

Cheshire

LEE, Michael: Astrology. Postal readings only.

Address: 18 Pembry Close, Brinnington, Stockport, Cheshire.

WILCOCK, Joseph William: Astrology. Postal readings only. Readings are (1) comprehensive birth chart; (2) birth chart plus analysis; (3) future trends (2 years).

Address: 27 Victoria Road, Woodbank, Offerton, Stockport.
Tel: (061) 428 3600 ext. 3094 between 9am and 4.30pm.

Cleveland

ZENA, Madame: Clairvoyance, numerology and Tarot. Private and postal readings.

Address: 55 West Dyke Road, Redcar, Cleveland.
Tel: (0642) 482045

Cornwall

TRUSCOTT, La Verne: Clairvoyance and healing. Postal readings only.

Address: Pencalenick Lodge, Thatched Cottage, St Clements, Truro, Cornwall.
Tel: (087252) 309

Devon

FRONTERAS, Adam, BAPS: Astrology, Tarot, I-Ching and crystal. Private and postal consultations plus a 'Tarot evening' for groups. Adam Fronteras is the regular astrologer for the *North Devon Advertiser*. He has appeared on London Weekend Television, Television South and BBC Radio One.

Address: Stoney Barton, Westleigh, Instow, Near Bideford, North Devon.
Tel: (0271) 860460

JAMES, Carol E: Clairvoyance, clairaudience, crystal and healing. Private and postal readings plus travel. Lectures and demonstrations suitable for either secular or spiritual gatherings. Classes in meditation, spiritual awareness, etc.

Address: Enlea Lodge, Newton Road, Kings Kerswell, Newton Abbot, Devon.
Tel: (08047) 2319

LE BEARN, Mrs Eileen: Clairvoyance, Greater World registered medium. Mrs Le Bearn is based in the Plymouth area and also serves churches.

Tel: (0752) 706571

MOORE, Jill, DF Astrol S: Astrology, Tarot and yoga. Private and postal readings plus travel. Also lectures and classes. Jill Moore is, in addition, a trained counsellor and a qualified yoga teacher. She writes regular feature articles for *Prediction* and she has also begun broadcasting on Devonair Radio.

Address: The Jill Moore School of Astrology, Victorian Arcade, Torwood Street, Torquay, Devon.
Tel: (0803) 22700

Dorset

ARNOLD, Jean: This medium specializes in psychic portraits: 'coloured portraits of those linked with you spiritually'.

Address: 268 Ilford Lane, Southbourne, Bournemouth, Dorset.
Tel: (0202) 429742

PAYNE, Mrs Evelyn: Clairvoyance, clairaudience and trance. Private consultations and travel by arrangement. Churches served.

Address: 8 West Mansions, 40 Poole Road, Bournemouth, Dorset.
Tel: (0202) 760352

Essex

CLARK, Fred: Greater World Registered Medium. Clairvoyance. Private readings plus travel. Churches served anywhere.

Address: 15 Ullswater Way, Elm Park, Hornchurch, Essex.
Tel: Hornchurch 55687

COHEN, Harold: Clairvoyance, clairaudience and healing. Private consultations only.

Address: 31 Bathurst Road, Ilford, Essex.
Tel: (01) 554 4084

DUNHAM, Julie: Astrology. Private and postal readings. Travels sometimes.

Address: Shrublands, Bradfield Road, Wix, Manningtree, Essex.

HANCOCK, Mrs Rita: Clairvoyance and clairaudience. She also specializes in spiritual psychology and psychic experiences. Private consultations.

Address: 59 St Albans Road, Woodford Green, Essex.
Tel: (01) 505 3095

LANE, Marguerita: Clairvoyance and clairaudience. Private consultations by appointment only.

Address: 11 Meath Road, Ilford, Essex.
Tel: (01) 478 7115

LILLEY, Richard, DMS Astrol: Astrology. Private and postal readings. Character analysis, future trends, synastry (comparison of two charts), birth chart calculations, vocational guidance and child's analysis.

Address: 52 Knox Road, Clacton, Essex.
Tel: (0255) 427981

PHIPPS, Lilian: Clairvoyance. Postal readings only. Postal readings are limited; enquiries by letter or telephone.

Address: 4a Argyll Road, Westcliff-on-Sea, Essex.
Tel: (0702) 352549

PRICE, Rosemary, PASS BAPS: Tarot and numerology. Private and postal consultations. Rosemary Price founded The Psychic and Allied Sciences Society, in August 1982. This organization holds socials, lectures, evening classes and has a register of qualified, tested consultants, proficient in all psychic and allied subjects. Enquiries for membership details must be accompanied by a stamped and self-addressed envelope.

Address: 43 Chester Road, Seven Kings, Ilford, Essex.
Tel: (01) 599 6013

SHIRL: Clairvoyance, clairaudience, palmistry, cartomancy (using standard cards), crystal and tea leaves. Private readings and travel for the purpose of group sittings and exhibitions. She is also a healer. Press and radio coverage.

Address: 1 Fitzwalter Road, Boreham, Near Chelmsford, Essex.
Tel: (0245) 467678

Gloucestershire

PARKER, Colin: Astrology. Private and postal consultations. Colin Parker is a tutor of the Mayo School of Astrology and also a BAPS consultant.

Address: 4 Westfield Terrace, Longford, Gloucester, Gloucestershire.

Hampshire

ANDERSON, Dorrach: Clairvoyance and numerology. Private and telephone consultations. Dorrach Anderson is a trance medium and she has been psychic all her life, coming from a family that produces a psychically-gifted child in every other generation on the maternal side.

Tel: Alton (0420) 84866

DYLIS, Louise: Tarot and psychometry. Private and postal readings.

Address: Highclere, Markson Road, South Wonston, Hampshire.
Tel: (0962) 883167

MARGARET: Astrology. Postal only. An astrologer of twenty years' experience, who aims to help clients to find their own way through an understanding of their horoscopes.

Address: 25 Birch Road, Headley, Bordon, Hants.

Hertfordshire

HOWARD, Mary: Clairvoyance, clairaudience, psychometry, astrology and Tarot. She is also a trance medium. Private readings only. She has diplomas in Psychic Science, Astrology and Tarot.

Address: 16 Jennings Road, St Albans, Herts.
Tel: (0727) 64939

Isle of Man

HOWDEN, Miss Ray: Clairvoyance and clairaudience. Private consultations and travel. This medium is a diploma holder who, apart from private readings, also works for the Spiritualist Association of Great Britain.

Address: Bengairn, 12 Queen's Drive West, Ramsey, Isle of Man.
Tel: (0624) 813173

Isle of Wight

FOSTER, Mrs Margaret: Contact and absent healing for cats and dogs. Mrs Foster receives absent healing requests from many overseas pet owners, particularly from such countries as Australia, South Africa, Sweden, the United States and Zimbabwe.

Address: 9 Nodgham Lane, Carisbrooke, Newport, Isle of Wight.
Tel: (0983) 522292

Kent

ANNE: Clairvoyance, palmistry. Personal and postal readings plus travel for group readings in homes. Anne has also established a reputation as a business consultant.

Address: 29 High Street, Maidstone, Kent.
Tel: (0622) 683726

CRANE, Gerard J, MFPhy LCSP(Assoc): Tarot. Private consultations. Gerard Crane is also a contact and absent spiritual healer who will travel to give healing but only to the disabled or housebound. He lists remedial massage and reflexology as his specialities.

Address: The Mayors Arms, 63 The Street, Ospringe, Faversham, Kent.
Tel: (0795) 532037

CRANE, Pamela, DF Aastol S DMS Astrol (Hon.) DPCC Horos: Astrology and Tarot. Private and postal consultations. Pamela Crane also teaches (privately and by correspondence), writes articles, gives talks including radio and television appearances, and she gives contact and absent spiritual healing. She will only travel to give healing to the disabled or housebound.

Address: Pamela Crane College of Horoscopy, The Mayors Arms, 63 The Street, Ospringe, Faversham, Kent.
Tel: (0795) 532037

EVELYN: Astrologer. Postal only.

Address: 2 Grosvenor Road, Upper Belvedere, Kent.

DIXON, Ron and Frances: Clairvoyance, clairaudience, numerology, Tarot and healing. Apart from private and postal consultations, Ron and Frances Dixon are the organizers of the Kent Psychic Groups, a kindred body of the SNU. They also run a separate psychic research project called Triline Research.

Address: 7 Alma road, Herne Bay, Kent.
Tel: (02273) 66038

DUBUISSON, Patrick H, BAPS: Astrology. Postal consultations.

Address: Flat 3, The Lantern Hotel, Hilltop, Charing, Kent.
Tel: (023371) 3261

GORDON, Keith: Clairvoyance, astrology and Tarot. Private, group and postal consultations plus travel. Apart from private work, Keith Gordon teaches and lectures. He is a member of BAPS.

Address: Fleur de Lis, 10 St Stephens Road, Canterbury, Kent.
Tel: (0227) 65054

KIERA: Clairvoyance, astrology, Tarot, crystal, sand, I-Ching, palmistry and tuition. Private and postal readings and travel.

Address: 207 High Street, Bromley, Kent.
Tel: (01) 681 3987/ 464 8812

MARA: Clairvoyance and psychometry. Private and postal readings plus travel. Private consultations by appointment only. Postal enquirers must enclose a stamped and self-addressed envelope.

Address: 32 Watling Street, Gillingham, Kent.
Tel: (0634) 56048

MANOUKA: Clairvoyance and Tarot. Private and postal consultations plus party bookings.

Address: 19 Yew Tree Close, Chatham, Kent.
Tel: (0634) 683566

MATTMAN, Frederick: Clairvoyance and healing. Private readings and local travel. Healing free by appointment. Local church served.

Address: 5 Sanctuary Road, Gillingham, Kent.
Tel: (0634) 373265

NAYLOR, John (ORION of the *Daily Mail*): Astrology. Postal only. Specializes in astrological features for newspapers and magazines.

Address: Skerry Vore, Undercliff, Sandgate, Folkestone, Kent.
Tel: (0303) 38178

PHILLIPA: Tarot and palmistry. Private and postal readings plus Tarot parties. Comprehensive hand print analysis. Private consultations combine palm and Tarot readings.

Address: Manor Cottage, Cherry Lane, Great Mongeham, Deal, Kent.
Tel: (03045) 2087

SALLY: Clairvoyance. Medium Sally Enness gives private and group consultations by appointment.

Address: The Old Coach House, Rocks Road, East Malling, Near Maidstone, Kent.
Tel: (0732) 843902

TRACEY, Kim: Runes, clairvoyance, clairaudience, psychometry and Tarot. Private and postal consultations plus postal Runecasts. Kim Tracey spends much of her time fulfilling engagements, both private and public, in Medway, London, Amsterdam and Beverly Hills. The rest of her time is spent writing. This clairvoyant was born with strong psychic gifts and she has led a dramatic and unusual life since early childhood. Her life story has been chronicled in *Secrets of the Runes*, published by Sphere Books in 1979. She has received extensive British, Dutch and American media coverage including guest spots on most TV and radio stations in this country. All enquiries should be conveyed to Dallas Lee.

Address: 42 Melville Court, Chatham, Kent.
Tel: (0634) 401168

WHEATLEY, Ron: Tarot and aurographs. Private and postal readings; also healing, lectures and courses. Travel.

Address: 28 Park View Road, Welling, Kent.
Tel: (01) 303 6154

Lancashire

DION, Christian: Clairvoyance, Tarot and crystal. Private and postal readings. He has travelled around the world, working in Australia and America. Featured on BBC TV. International clientele. Groups.

Address: PO Box SSBO 16, Blackpool, Lancashire.
Tel: (0253) 593433

GARDNER, Edna: Clairvoyance, clairaudience. Private consultations and travel.

Address: 145 Chorley Road, Westhoughton, Near Bolton, Lancashire.
Tel: (0942) 814207

RATCLIFFE, Mrs G: Clairvoyance, crystal and psychometry. Private and postal readings.

Address: 26 Carlton Gardens, Farnworth, Bolton, Lancashire.
Tel: (0204) 76159

REEVES, Sheila: Originally a London-based medium. Private and postal readings; also travel and healing.

Address: 27 Sheridan Road, Laneshaw Bridge, Colne, Lancashire.
Tel: (0282) 865606

Leicestershire

COOPER, Christine: Clairvoyance and Tarot. Private and postal consultations.

Address: 93 Heyford Road, Braunstone Estate, Leicester.
Tel: (0533) 857672

COOPER, Paul Gary: Clairvoyance. Private and postal consultations.

Address: 93 Heyford Road, Braunstone Estate, Leicester 3.
Tel: (0533) 857672

JEVON, Denis: Numerology and Tarot. He also uses the runes and practises psychometry. Private and postal readings. Appointment by telephone. As a psychic consultant, he covers all aspects of life – health, marital, business, etc.

Address: 79 Buckingham Drive, Thorpe Acre, Loughborough, Leicestershire.
Tel: (0509) 267232

NICHOLS, Jane: Clairvoyance, auric readings and flowergraphs. Postal readings only. She also serves churches and teaches spiritual philosophy.

Address: 123 Gipsy Lane, Leicester 4.

RUSH, Ms, M: Astrology. Private readings by prior appointment only. Also talks to groups, societies, etc., on astrology, handwriting analysis and numerology.

Address: 26 Nene Drive, Oadby, Leicester.
Tel: (0533) 716827

TEASDALE, Mrs Florence Beatrice: Clairvoyance, clairaudience, philosophy and flower service. Mrs Teasdale only serves churches. She anticipates being able to travel outside her local area in the near future. Her flower service involves each member of the congregation being asked to bring a flower with him or her. The flowers are then placed on a tray which is kept out of Mrs Teasdale's view. At the appropriate time, this medium proceeds to pick up individual flowers, as instructed by spirit, and passes messages to the donors, not knowing beforehand who has given which flower.

Address: 12a Green Lane Close, Seagrave, Near Loughborough, Leicestershire.
Tel: (050981) 4693

Lincolnshire

DALE, Annie: Clairvoyance, astrology and crystal. Private and postal readings. She will travel reasonable distances to lecture. She teaches astrology, meditation, self-hypnosis and also advises on health and fitness. She is available for fund-raising events which aid children, animals, the handicapped and all those seeking God through various paths of life.

Address: The Haven, 5 Links Avenue, Mablethorpe, Lincolnshire.
Tel: (05213) 7794

REGGIE: Clairvoyance, trance and crystal. Private and postal consultations.

Address: 8 Shakespeare Street, Lincoln, Lincolnshire.
Tel: (0522) 33023

ROSE, Madame: Clairvoyance, clairaudience and Tarot. Known as the Queen of the Tarot Cards, Madame Rose also uses her other gifts to prove survival to bereaved clients and to help with birth predictions for childless couples. As well as being an authoress, she has had extensive media coverage including an in-depth interview which appeared in *My Weekly*. Private and postal readings. A catalogue of psychic services is available by post. Please write enclosing four first-class stamps.

Address: 4 Burton Avenue, Rainhill, Merseyside.
Tel: (051) 426 5741

Middlesex

ANAND, Jyotishi (P A Patel): Astrology, palmistry, numerology and Tarot. Private and postal readings. He uses Western as well as Hindu systems of astrology.

Address: 8 Cecil Avenue, Wembley, Middlesex.
Tel: (01) 903 6784

BENNET, Mrs Eve: Clairvoyance and clairaudience. Private and postal readings. This medium will travel to give readings if the location is within or near her home area.

Address: 133 Lansbury Drive, Hayes, Middlesex.
Tel: (01) 561 6652

JAMES, Ernie: Clairvoyance, clairaudience, numerology, astrology, Tarot, crystal, sand, aurographs and healing. Private and postal readings plus travel. Mr James also teaches the psychic arts.

Address: 3 Chandos Road, Staines, Middlesex.
Tel: (0784) 59669

POTA, Mrs B P: Palmistry and astrology (mainly Hindu astrology). Private and postal consultations. Private consultations by appointment. Mrs Pota will also give advice over the telephone, after receiving questions by post from clients.

Address: 6 Ruskin Gardens, Kenton, Middlesex.
Tel: (01) 204 2352

Norfolk

ANDRED: Clairvoyance and numerology. Postal readings plus travel. This psychic consultant also has available auric self-development cassettes on meditation, astral projection and all subjects of the psyche.

Address: 17 Brampton Court, Clover Hill, Bowthorpe, Norwich, Norfolk.

GIBBARD, Mike: Clairvoyance and clairaudience. Private, postal readings and travel. He regularly visits London. Contact and absent healing also given.

Address: 8 Redmere Close, Frettenham, Norwich, Norfolk.
Tel: (0603) 737081

Northumberland

PURVIS, Janis: Clairvoyance, clairaudience, astrology, runes (postal). Private, postal cassette readings and absent healing. Spirit inspired messages of a philosophical nature are taped when in trance.

Address: 105 Avebury Place, Eastfield Lea, Cramlington, Northumberland.
Tel: (0670) 733141

WADE, Myrna: Clairvoyance, Tarot and crystal. Private and postal readings plus travel. Myrna is also a faith healer.

Address: 10 Yeovil Close, Westwood Grange, Cramlington, Northumberland.
Tel: (0670) 712217

Nottinghamshire

LANCASHIRE, Linda: Clairaudience, numerology, astrology, Tarot, crystal, palmistry and psychometry. Private readings plus travel. Guest appearances on BBC Radio and BBC Television. This psychic is a newspaper and magazine writer of prolific output.

Address: 16 Sutton Road, Kirkby-in-Ashfield, Nottinghamshire.
Tel: (0623) 757900

LING, Gienieve Margret: Clairvoyance and cartomancy. Postal readings only.

Address: 21 Brierfield Avenue, Wilford, Nottingham.
Tel: (0602) 813049

Oxfordshire

THEODOROU, Patricia, BAPS: Astrology. Private and postal consultations. Patricia Theodorou's interest in astrology goes back to the age of thirteen. She is particularly interested in working with aptitude analysis, children's charts and vocational guidance. She will also undertake any general enquiry: chart comparisons, hororay astrology, etc.

Address: 23 Church Street, Henley-on-Thames, Oxon.
Tel: (04912) 78335

Somerset

ELLIOT, Roger: Astrology. Private, telephone and cassette consultations.

Address: The Manor, Crossington, Bridgwater, Somerset.
Tel: (0278) 722764

Staffordshire

HARNETT, Liz: Clairvoyance, astrology, Tarot, I-Ching, psychometry and gravel reading (interpretation not read aloud). Private and postal consultations.

Address: 4 Java Crescent, Trentham, Stoke-on-Trent, Staffordshire.
Tel: (0782) 642637

KILNER, Eileen: Clairvoyance, clairaudience and flower sentience. Eileen Kilner is a Greater World registered medium and is also a member of the Institute of Spiritualists. She serves churches in Nottinghamshire, Derbyshire, Leicestershire, Lancashire, Staffordshire, Huntingdon and Sussex.

Address: Birdwood, Tutbury Road, Rural, Burton-on-Trent, Staffordshire.

NICHOLAS, Brian Maylett: Clairvoyance. Private and postal readings plus travel within a reasonable distance. He is also a healer, helping people with physical and mental conditions. He does this through his readings. Apart from private consultations, he also gives lectures and holds discussions on clairvoyance and healing.

Address: 83 Wigginton Road, Tamworth, Staffordshire.
Tel: (0827) 4474

OCALLABAR: Clairvoyance. Private and postal readings.

Address: 41 High Street, Newhall, Burton-on-Trent, Staffordshire.
Tel: (0283) 213515

Suffolk

OPFER, Duskrainer and Albert, CHP DHP MAHP: Clairvoyance, clairaudience, numerology, Tarot and crystal. The Opfers are also hypnotherapists and psychotherapists, as well as being psychic consultants. They travel for demonstrations and lectures on all psychic subjects. Relaxation tapes made to individual requirements for progression, astral travel, etc.

Address: 104 London Road, Ipswich, Suffolk.
Tel: (0473) 56933

Surrey

AQUA: Clairvoyance, clairaudience, Tarot, psychometry and cartomancy. Private and postal readings, also travel. Parties attended. Free healing.

Address: 51 Derby Road, West Croydon, Surrey.
Tel: (01) 681 7015

AQUARIUS: Clairvoyance, clairaudience, astrology, crystal and dowsing. Only occasional travel. Lectures on astrology and dowsing. She also uses the pendulum for tracing missing animals such as cats.

Address: 21 Hardman Road, Kingston, Surrey.
Tel: (01) 548 2380

SASHA: Clairvoyance, clairaudience, astrology. Tarot, palmistry and some psychometry. Private and postal readings plus travel.

Address: 21 Warnham Court Road, Carshalton Beeches, Surrey.
Tel: (01) 643 2293

WINTER, Mrs Rosemary: Clairvoyance, psychometry, flower psychometry and sand reading. Private and group consultations. Mrs Winter is also a spiritual healer and a member of the Surrey Healers' Group. Apart from her private and group activities, this medium also takes church services.

Address: 15 Holm Court, Flint Hill, Dorking, Surrey.
Tel: (0306) 880701

Sussex

LEGGE, Gladys and David: Clairvoyance. Private and postal readings plus travel. Gladys and David work together as clairvoyant mediums.

Address: 21 Blackdown Road, Durrington, Worthing, West Sussex.
Tel: (0903) 67904

RALSTON, Jenny: Tarot, spiritual healing. Private and postal appointments. Local travel.

Address: 4 Blackbird Hill, Turners Hill, Near Crawley, West Sussex.
Tel: (0342) 715732

SANDERS, Gregory: Astrology. Private and postal readings.

Address: 16 Stuart Avenue, Eastbourne, Sussex.

VERENA: Tarot and standard playing cards. Private consultations and travel if need be.

Address: Two Gates, Gillham Wood Avenue, Cooden, Bexhill-on-Sea, East Sussex.
Tel: (04243) 5263

Tyne & Wear

SIAN, Madam: Clairvoyance, astrology, crystal and cartomancy. Private and postal readings. She gives yearly forecasts to newspapers and radio.

Address: 60 Hyde Park Street, Gateshead, Tyne & Wear.
Tel: (0632) 782630

West Midlands

JOHN: Tarot and astrology. Private and postal readings.

Address: 75 Hollemeadow Avenue, Leamore, Walsall, West Midlands.
Tel: (0922) 75184

Yorkshire

ABBOTT, Myra: Clairvoyance, clairaudience and diagnostic healing. Private and postal consultations plus travel. This medium also takes development, discussion and healing groups and organizes psychic workshops. In addition to this, she still finds time to serve churches.

Address: 13 Northumberland Road, Sheffield, South Yorkshire.
Tel: (0742) 737077

BRIDGFORD, Mrs Barbara S: Clairvoyance. Private and postal consultations, plus appointments for private healing. There is also healing on Tuesday afternoons at 2pm for which no appointment is necessary.

Address: Tarrock, Parish Ghyll Drive, Ilkley, West Yorkshire.
Tel: (0943) 601872

HUMPHRIES, Mrs Kathleen: Clairvoyance, clairaudience. Private and postal readings.

Address: 6 Danum Road, Broadway, York.
Tel: (0904) 35506

PAULINE, Madam: Clairvoyance and clairaudience. Postal only.

Address: 4 St Margaret's Court, Illingworth, Halifax, West Yorkshire.

SPEIGHT, Freddie: Clairvoyance, numerology and Tarot. Private and postal readings. Private readings by appointment only. Also long reading facility with tape included. Talismans can be made to order. Date of birth and colouring required for all work.

Address: Meadow Bank, 129 Luck Lane, Paddock, Huddersfield, Yorkshire.
Tel: (0484) 42153

VAN ZYL, Gabrielle: Clairvoyance, Tarot, crystal, I-Ching, pendulum and psychometry. These are just some of the methods of divination used by Gabrielle, an ex-university administrator who is now a full-time psychic. She was born with psychic gifts and has made in-depth studies of the occult and psychic arts. Postal readings only.

Address: Bardon Grange Lodge, 103 Weetwood Lane, Leeds.

Scotland

CAMERON, James: Clairvoyance, numerology, Tarot and graphology. Postal consultations only. James Cameron is director of The Prayer Power Fellowship.

Address: Cloich-mhile, Stanley, Perth, Scotland.

WILLMOTT, John: Private and postal consultations. This astrologer also runs an astrology school.

Address: Tiroran, Isle of Mull, Argyll, Scotland.
Tel: (06815) 252

Wales

BROWN, Edna: Clairvoyance. Strictly postal consultations only. Please enclose a stamped and self-addressed envelope for a reply.

Address: 137 St Fagans Road, Fairwater, Cardiff, Wales.

CRASZWELL, Chryss, DMS Astrol: Astrology and counselling through spirit. Chryss Craszwell and his group comprise five adults and two children. He states: 'We are beginning a spiritual community based on astrology and spiritual growth.'

Address: Galactic Federation HQ, Tyn-y-Felin, Llanrhyddlad, Anglesey, Gwynedd.

DU MAURIER, Mary, BA: Clairvoyance, clairaudience, astrology, Tarot, runes and biorhythms. Postal readings and preparations of talismans. Also travel. Mary du Maurier offers a high quality consultation service and replies are sent within twenty-eight days.

Address: The Cedars, 58 Colchester Avenue, Penylan, Cardiff, Wales.

EDWIN, E: Clairvoyance, psychometry, healing and

absent healing. Private and home visits for healing appointments.

Address: 45 Oaklands Terrace, Gilfynydd, Pontypridd, Mid Glamorgan, South Wales.
Tel: (0443) 403097

HUMPHREYS, Margaret: Clairvoyance and clairaudience. Postal readings and limited private readings.

Address: 106a Stanwell Road, Penarth, South Glamorgan.
Tel: (0222) 703126

KARMA: Clairvoyance. Postal only.

Address: 157 Upper Mostyn Street, Llandudno, Gwynedd, North Wales.

LOCKE, Claudia: Clairvoyance, clairaudience, astrology and healing. Private and postal consultations plus travel.

Address: Pencarniced, Tregrose, Llandysul, Dyfed, Wales.
Tel: (055932) 3543

LOCKE, Paula: Clairvoyance, clairaudience and some astrology. Paula Locke is also a lecturer and teacher of spiritual philosophy. Private and postal consultations plus travel.

Address: Pencarniced, Tregrose, Llandysul, Dyfed, Wales.
Tel: (055932) 3543

TALBOT, Sheila: Astrology. Postal only.

Address: 4 Chapel Close, Aberthin, Cowbridge, South Glamorgan.
Tel: (04463) 2712

VIOLET: Clairvoyance and numerology. Postal readings only.

Address: 40 Birkdale Avenue, Colwyn Bay, Clwyd, North Wales.
Tel: (0492) 33229

Northern Ireland

FARMER, Hamilton: Clairvoyance, clairaudience and astrology. Lectures and classes on development and other psychic subjects. He also undertakes church work, giving lectures and demonstrations. Frequent media coverage including appearances on BBC TV's *Nationwide* and Ulster Region TV. A successful lecture and demonstration tour in California is to be followed by a similar tour in the same area. Private and postal readings plus travel.

Address: 75 Great Victoria Street, Belfast 2, Northern Ireland.
Tel: (0232) 2200071

Methods of Divination Practised by Listed Consultants

Consultants are listed alphabetically under each heading and their city or county location is located alongside in brackets.

Only the main systems of divination are listed in this index; therefore readers are advised to read each consultant's profile for full information.

The methods of divination listed here are:

ASTROLOGY
CARTOMANCY
CLAIRAUDIENCE
CLAIRVOYANCE
CRYSTAL
I-CHING
NUMEROLOGY
PALMISTRY
PSYCHOMETRY
RUNES
TAROT

Astrology

Anand, Jyotoshi
   (Middlesex)
Aquarius (Surrey)
Augustus, John (London)
Brady, Julia (London)
Carole and Norman
   (London)

Crane, Pamela (Kent)
Craszwell, Chryss
   (Gwynedd, Wales)
Dale, Annie (Lincolnshire)
Davies, Fredrick (London
   & New York)
Dubuisson, Patrick (Kent)

Du Maurier, Mary
(Cardiff, Wales)
Elliot, Roger (Somerset)
Evelyn (Kent)
Farmer, Hamilton (Belfast,
N Ireland)
Fronteras, Adam (Devon)
Gainey (London)
Ghani, M A (London)
Gordon, Keith (Kent)
Harlequin, The (London)
Harnett, Liz
(Staffordshire)
James (London)
James, Ernie (Middlesex)
John (West Midlands)
Kaz (London)
Kiera (Kent)
Lancashire, Linda
(Nottinghamshire)
Lee, Michael (Cheshire)
Lilley, Richard (Essex)
Locke, Claudia (Dyfed,
Wales)
Locke, Paula (Dyfed,
Wales)
Margaret (Hampshire)

Moore, Jill (Devon)
Naylor, John – Orion of
the *Daily Mail* (Kent)
Parker, Colin
(Gloucestershire)
Pota, B P (Middlesex)
Potts, Sue (London)
Purvis, Janis
(Northumberland)
Rachael, Jane (London)
Roebuck, Charles, W
(Manchester)
Rush, M (Leicestershire)
Sasha (Surrey)
Saunders, Gregory
(Sussex)
Talbot, Sheila (Cowbridge,
Wales)
Theodorou, Patricia
(Oxfordshire)
Warick, J (Liverpool)
Wilcock, Joseph William
(Cheshire)
Willmott, John (Isle of
Mull)
Wilson, Carole E
(Glasgow)

Cartomancy (see also: *Tarot*)

Aqua (Surrey)
Ellis, Dawn (London)
Jehane (Bedfordshire)
Ling, Geinieve Margret
(Nottinghamshire)
Parsons, Robert A
(London)

Shirl (Essex)
Sian, Madam (Tyne &
Wear)
Varena (Essex)
Warick, J (Liverpool)

Clairaudience

Abbott, Myra, (Yorkshire)
Aqua (Surrey)
Aquarius (Surrey)
Baizley, G (London)
Baker, Joyce (Cornwall)
Barham, Irene (London)
Brady, Julia (London)
Brough-Eley, Leslie
  (London)
Cohen, Harold (London)
Collins, Ziata (London)
Crystal-Broadwood, Sylvia
  (London)
Dixon, Ron and Frances
  (Kent)
Dougal, Alan (London)
Du Maurier, Mary
  (Cardiff, Wales)
Everett, Lee (London)
Farmer, Hamilton (Belfast,
  N Ireland)
Gardner, Edna
  (Lancashire)
Garman, Joan (London)
Gibbard, Mike (Norfolk)
Hancock, Rita (Essex)
Harlequin, The (London)
Howard, Mary
  (Hertfordshire)
Howden, Miss Ray (Isle of
  Man)
Humphreys, Margaret
  (Penarth, Wales)
Humphries, Kathleen
  (Yorkshire)
Jackson, Wendy (London)
James, Carol E (Devon)

James, Ernie (Middlesex)
Kilner, Eileen
  (Staffordshire)
Lancashire, Linda (Notts)
Lane, Marguerita (Essex)
Lawrence, Dr Richard H
  (London)
Lena (London)
Lester, Aislinn (London)
Locke, Paula (Dyfed,
  Wales)
Muriel (London)
Parsons, Robert A
  (London)
Pauline, Madame
  (Yorkshire)
Payne, Evelyn (Dorset)
Pearse, Lilian (London)
Potts, Owen (London)
Rae, Margaret (London)
Rose, Madame
  (Merseyside)
Sasha (Surrey)
Shirl (Essex)
Starkey, John
  (Birmingham)
Starr, Liliane Mitchell
  (Liverpool)
Teasdale, Florence
  Beatrice (Leicestershire)
Terry (London)
Tracey, Kim (Kent)
Ubels, Edward (London)
Yasmine (London)
Young, Millicent
  (Berkshire)

Abbott, Myra (Yorkshire)
Anderson, Dorrach
(Hampshire)
Andred (Norfolk)
Aqua (Surrey)
Aquarius (Surrey)
Augustus, John (London)
Anne (Kent)
Baizley, G (London)
Baker, Joyce (Cornwall)
Barham, Irene (London)
Brace, Louise (London)
Brady, Julia (London)
Brough-Eley, Leslie
(London)
Cameron, James (Perth,
Scotland)
Cephas, Peter
(Bedfordshire)
Clark, Fred (Essex)
Cohen, Harold (London)
Collins, Ziata (London)
Cooper, Christine
(Leicestershire)
Cooper, Paul Gary
(Leicestershire)
Crystal-Broadwood, Sylvia
(London)
Dabrowa, Betty (London)
Dale, Annie (Lincolnshire)
Dann-Szulc, Eileen
(Middlesex)
Davies, Fredrick (London
& New York)
Dion, Christian
(Lancashire)

Dixon, Ron and Frances
(Kent)
Dougal, Alan (London)
Du Maurier, Mary
(Cardiff, Wales)
Edwin, E (South Wales)
Ellis, Dawn (London)
Everett, Lee (London)
Farmer, Hamilton (Belfast,
N Ireland)
Gainey (London)
Gardner, Edna
(Lancashire)
Garman, Joan (London)
Gibbard, Mike (Norfolk)
Gordon, Keith (Kent)
Hancock, Rita (Essex)
Harlequin, The (London)
Harnett, Liz
(Staffordshire)
Holland, Mary Selina
(Yorkshire)
Howard, Mary
(Hertfordshire)
Howarth, Sybil (London)
Howden, Miss Ray (Isle of
Man)
Homewood, Elizabeth
(Surrey)
Humphreys, Margaret
(Penarth, Wales)
Humphries, Kathleen
(Yorkshire)
Jackson, Wendy (London)
James, Carol E (Devon)
James, Ernie (Middlesex)

Karma (Gwynedd, Wales)
Kiera (Kent)
Kilner, Eileen
   (Staffordshire)
Lane, Marguerita (Essex)
Larno, A (London)
   Lawrence, Dr Richard
   H (London)
Legge, Gladys & David
   (Sussex)
Lena (London)
Lester, Aislinn (London)
Ling, Geinieve Margret
   (Nottinghamshire)
Locke, Claudia (Dyfed,
   Wales)
Locke, Paula (Dyfed,
   Wales)
Luxon, Bettina (London)
Manouka (Kent)
Mara (Kent)
Mattman, Frederick
   (Kent)
Muriel (London)
Mussell, Derek (London)
Nicholas, Brian Maylett
   (Staffordshire)
Nicholls, Jane
   (Leicestershire)
Ocallabar (Staffordshire)
Opfer, Duskrainer and
   Albert (Suffolk)
Pandya, Ashwin (London)
Parsons, Robert A.
   (London)
Pauline, Madame
   (Yorkshire)
Payne, Evelyn (Dorset)
Pearse, Lilian (London)

Phipps, Lilian (Essex)
Player, Kathryn (London)
Potts, Owen (London)
Potts, Sue (London)
Purvis, Janis
   (Northumberland)
Rae, Margaret (London)
Ratcliffe, Mrs G
   (Lancashire)
Reeves, Sheila
   (Lancashire)
Reggie (Lincolnshire)
Rose, Madame
   (Merseyside)
Sally (Kent)
Sasha (Surrey)
Shirl (Essex)
Sian, Madam (Tyne &
   Wear)
Speight, Freddie
   (Yorkshire)
Starr, Liliane Mitchell
   (Liverpool)
Staves, Marjorie (London)
Teasdale, Florence
   Beatrice (Leicestershire)
Terry (London)
Theodora, Madame
   (London)
Tracey, Kim (Kent)
Truscott, La Verne
   (Cornwall)
Van Zyl, Gabrielle
   (Yorkshire)
Violet (Colwyn Bay, Wales)
Wade, Myrna
   (Northumberland)
Winter, Rosemary (Surrey)
Yasmine (London)

Young, Millicent
  (Berkshire)

Zena, Madame
  (Cleveland)

Crystal

Aquarius (Surrey)
Augustus, John (London)
Dale, Annie (Lincolnshire)
Dion, Christian
  (Lancashire)
Fronteras, Adam (Devon)
Harlequin, The (London)
Howarth, Sybil (London)
James, Carol E (Devon)
James, Ernie (Middlesex)
Kaz (London)
Kiera (Kent)
Lancashire, Linda
  (Nottinghamshire)
Larno A (London)

Lawrence, Dr Richard H
  (London)
Lester, Aislinn (London)
Ratcliffe, Mrs G
  (Lancashire)
Reggie (Lincolnshire)
Shirl (Essex)
Sian, Madam (Tyne &
  Wear)
Theodora, Madame
  (London)
Van Zyl, Gabrielle
  (Yorkshire)
Wade, Myrna
  (Northumberland)

I-Ching

Fronteras, Adam (Devon)
Harnett, Liz
  (Staffordshire)
Ingmar, Madam (London)
Kaz (London)
Kiera (Kent)

Lester, Aislinn (London)
Van Zyl, Gabrielle
  (Yorkshire)
Wood, Glorie (London)
Yasmine (London)

Numerology

Anand, Jyotoshi
  (Middlesex)
Anderson, Dorrach
  (Hampshire)
Andred (Norfolk)

Augustus, John (London)
Cameron, James (Perth,
  Scotland)
Davies, Fredrick (London
  & New York)

Dixon, Ron and Frances (Kent)
Ghani, M A (London)
Harlequin, The (London)
Howarth, Sybil (London)
Jackson, Wendy (London)
James, Ernie (Middlesex)
Jevon, Denis (Leicestershire)
Kaz (London)
Lancashire, Linda (Nottinghamshire)
Lester, Aislinn (London)
Mamdani, Silim (London)

Opfer, Duskrainer and Albert (Suffolk)
Pandya, Ashwin (London)
Price, Rosemary (Essex)
Rush, M (Leicestershire)
Speight, Freddie (Yorkshire)
Terry (London)
Violet (Wales)
Warick, J (Liverpool)
Young, Millicent, M C (Berkshire)
Zena, Madame (Cleveland)

Palmistry

Acushla (Avon)
Anand, Jyotoshi (Middlesex)
Anderson, Keith (Avon)
Anne (Kent)
Bashir, Mir (London)
Jackson, Wendy (London)
Kiera (Kent)
Lancashire, Linda (Nottinghamshire)

Larno A (London)
Luxon, Bettina (London)
Mamdani, Salim (London)
Pandya, Ashwin (London)
Peplow, Patricia (London)
Phillipa (Kent)
Pota, B P (Middlesex)
Sasha (Surrey)
Shirl (Essex)

Psychometry

Aqua (Surrey)
Collins, Ziata (London)
Dylis, Louise (Hampshire)
Edwin, E (Wales)
Harnett, Liz (Staffordshire)
Howard, Mary (Hertfordshire)

Jevon, Denis (Leicestershire)
Lancashire, Linda (Nottinghamshire)
Lester, Aislinn (London)
Mara (Kent)
Ratcliffe, Mrs G (Lancashire)
Sasha (Surrey)

Starr, Liliane Mitchell
(Liverpool)
Tracey, Kim (Kent)

Van Zyl, Gabrielle
(Yorkshire)

Runes

Carole and Norman
(London)
Du Maurier, Mary (Wales)
Jevon, Denis
(Leicestershire)

Kaz (London)
Purvis, Janis
(Northumberland)
Tracey, Kim (Kent)

Tarot (see also: Cartomancy)

Acushla (Avon)
Anand, Jyotoshi
(Middlesex)
Aqua (Surrey)
Augustus, John (London)
Bourne, Brian (London)
Brady, Julie (London)
Cameron, James (Perth,
Scotland)
Carole and Norman
(London)
Cooper, Christine
(Leicestershire)
Crane, Gerard (Kent)
Crane, Pamela (Kent)
Davies, Fredrick (London
& New York)
Dion, Christian
(Lancashire)
Dixon, Ron and Frances
(Kent)
Du Maurier, Mary
(Cardiff, Wales)

Durnin, Jackie (London)
Dylis, Louise (Hampshire)
Fronteras, Adam (Devon)
Gordon, Keith (Kent)
Gradwell, Henry Stephen
(London)
Harlequin, The (London)
Harnett, Liz
(Staffordshire)
Howard, Mary
(Hertfordshire)
Howarth, Sybil (London)
Jackson, Wendy (London)
James (London)
James, Ernie (Middlesex)
Jevon, Denis
(Leicestershire)
John (West Midlands)
Kaz (London)
Kiera (Kent)
Lancashire, Linda
(Nottinghamshire)
Lena (London)

Lester, Aislinn (London)
Luxon, Bettina (London)
Manouka (Kent)
Moore, Jill (Devon)
Opfer, Duskrainer and
    Albert (Suffolk)
Peplow, Patricia (London)
Phillipa (Kent)
Player, Kathryn (London)
Potts, Owen (London)
Potts, Sue (London)
Price, Rosemary (Essex)
Rachael, Jane (London)
Ralston, Jenny (Sussex)
Roebuck, Charles W
    (Manchester)

Rose, Madame
    (Merseyside)
Sarenne (London)
Sasha (Surrey)
Speight, Freddie
    (Yorkshire)
Terry (London)
Tracey, Kim (Kent)
Ubels, Edward (London)
Van Zyl, Gabrielle
    (Yorkshire)
Varena (Sussex)
Wade, Myrna
    (Northumberland)
Wheatley, Ron (Kent)
Yasmine (London)
Zena, Madame (Cleveland)

Directory of Healers

London

COOMBS, Martin: Contact and absent healing. Also healing via the telephone. Martin Coombs travels and regularly gives talks and demonstrations. He has appeared as a radio guest and received national press coverage in 1979 when he went to the aid of a doomed horse and again in 1980–81, when various articles were published in connection with his healing of a baby girl.

Address: 8 Colfe Road, Forest Hill, London SE23.
Tel: (01) 291 1020

CRYSTAL-BROADWOOD, Mrs Sylvia: This healer and medium is President of the St Francis of Assisi Healing Sanctuary for animals. She is also a spiritual counsellor, clairvoyant, clairaudient and a practising professional medium at the Spiritualist Association of Great Britain. Contact and absent healing plus travel.

Address: 35a Winterstoke Road, London SE6.

FORDHAM, Roy Sydney NFSH DSNU: Contact and absent healing. He sometimes travels.

Address: 10 West Heath Road, Bostall Heath, Abbey Wood, London SE2.
Tel: (01) 310 5511

LEECH-SCHWERTZEL, Madame Nadine: Trance healer. Contact healing only. Member of the International Federation of Spiritual Healers.

Address: 25a Lithos Road, London NW3.
Tel: (01) 435 4773

MUSSELL, Derek: Healing and clairvoyance. Healing is his main service. Private consultations.

Tel: (01) 529 3657

STALLEY, Edwin: Contact and absent healing from a sanctuary.

Address: 338 Wickham Lane, London SE2.
Tel: (01) 854 5759

STALLEY, Ena: Contact and absent healing from a sanctuary.

Address: 338 Wickham Lane, London SE2.
Tel: (01) 854 5759

STURZAKER, Doreen L: Esoteric healer. Uses hands and colour healing technique. Private consultations by appointment. This healer is co-author of *Colour and Kabbalah*, and co-principal of the International Order of Kabbalists.

Address: 25 Circle Gardens, Merton Park, London SW19.
Tel: (01) 542 3611

TINGEY, Michael: Healing and reflexology. Contact and absent healing plus travel.

Address: 26 Boleyn Road, East Ham, London E6.
Tel: (01) 472 3079

Cornwall

BAKER, Joyce: Contact and absent healing plus travel. Joyce Baker is also a clairvoyant and clairaudient who has been a consultant on the advisory panel of a psychic publication.

Address: Chy Albeth, 5 Fore Street, Beacon, Camborne, Cornwall.
Tel: (0209) 714031

Devon

BURNARD, Mrs Barbara: Contact and absent healing. Mrs Burnard will visit hospitals and travel within reason. She places great value on talking to people about their problems and the importance of explaining the real reason for life. She does not charge a fee but donations are accepted.

Address: 25 Mylor Close, Pennycross, Plymouth, Devon.

HORNER, Irene: Healing and/or counselling. Private consultations. Please write in first instance for appointment. No charge is made for healing or counselling.

Address: 127d King Street Flats, Plymouth, Devon.

KING, Eve: Absent healing.

Address: 19 South Street, Exmouth, Devon.

PSYCHO EXPANSION CENTRE: Contact and absent healing, also spiritual development. Enquiries are welcome and should be made to Mr Barney Camfield or Mrs Valerie Gregory.

Address: 53 Amherst Road, Pennycomequick, Plymouth, Devon.
Tel: (0752) 667686

WYNDHAM, Phil and Kath: Contact and absent healing. Distant healing also given via the telephone. Contact healing is given from a healing sanctuary.

Address: Canberra, Dropwell Meadow, Torrington, Devon.
Tel: (08052) 2478

Hampshire

NOCK, Frederick Thomas: Contact and absent healing. Mr Nock is a trance healer and trance medium. Healing takes place at a sanctuary.

Address: Sanctuary, Zenith Art Centre, 891 Christchurch Road, Pokesdown, Bournemouth, Hampshire.
Tel: (0202) 425188

Hertfordshire

NEW BARNET HEALERS: Contact and absent healing. Contact healing every Wednesday, between 2pm and 8pm.

Tel: (01) 449 5670

WRIGHT, Ronald: Private, absent and church healing. He also gives healing to animals.

Address: 5 Mead Lane, Hertford, Hertfordshire.

Isle of Man

JENKINS, Janine and John, NFSH BSNU: Contact and absent healing. Healing also conducted at church.

Address: Temidayo, Endfield Avenue, Port St Mary, Isle of Man.

Kent

MATTMAN, Mrs Pat: Contact and absent healing. Please enclose a stamped and self-addressed envelope when writing for absent healing, enquiries, etc. Healing by appointment. No charge is made.

Address: 5 Sanctuary Road, Gillingham, Kent.
Tel: (0634) 373265

Lincolnshire

REEVE, Christopher A: Contact and absent healing. He will travel if necessary.

Address: 31 South Street, Bourne, Lincolnshire.
Tel: (07782) 3730

Middlesex

DANN-SZULC, Mrs Eileen CSNU: Contact and aura healing plus limited local travel for the benefit of the disabled. Mrs Dann-Szulc is also a clairvoyant and counsellor.

Address: 47 Bridgewater Road, Wembley, Middlesex.
Tel: (01) 902 9854

Norfolk

CONEY, John W G: Contact and absent healer who will also travel reasonable distances.

Address: Grange Lodge, Coast Road, Overstrand, Norfolk.
Tel: (026378) 645

Somerset

CARTER, Mrs Maria-Diana: Contact and absent healing. Animals are also given absent healing. This healer will travel if necessary.

Address: 31 Hamlyn Road, Glastonbury, Somerset.
Tel: (0458) 32799

OLD RING OF BELLS HEALING SANCTUARY: Contact and absent healing. The Old Ring of Bells was built as a monks' retreat during the fourteenth century. It rests in the midst of the Mendip Moors. Large grounds lead down to the River Brue. Facilities are available for healing vacations which, apart from the healing sessions, include bed and breakfast and an evening meal. For full details contact either Dennis Vink or Dudley E James.

Address: Old Ring of Bells Healing Sanctuary, Meare, Glastonbury, Somerset.
Tel: (04586) 635

PLUMLEY, Mr and Mrs M: NFS registered healers. Private appointments and calls made within a reasonable distance. No fees are charged for healing but donations are accepted to cover domestic running costs. Where travel is concerned, petrol expenses may be asked for, but only in exceptional circumstances.

Address: Southfield, 5 Cossington Lane, Woolavington, Bridgwater, Somerset.
Tel: (0278) 683362

Suffolk

HADLEIGH HEALING SOCIETY (registered charity): Involved in full-time healing and the teaching of psychic awareness. Membership of eighty people, many of whom are first-class psychics. All enquiries welcome.

Tel: (0473) 823282

Surrey

HOMEWOOD, Miss Elizabeth: Clairvoyance and trance used if necessary for the treatment of patients. This healer works with an alternative therapies clinic in New Malden, Surrey. Specialist healing lies with neuro/mental conditions, although general healing is undertaken. In-depth experience of obsessions, neurological diseases and allergies. This healer has recently retired from the Social Services. She hopes to impress upon them the importance of the areas of healing in which she works. She will travel to give lectures.

Address: 149 Tudor Drive, Kingston-upon-Thames, Surrey.
Tel: (01) 549 6584

PULLEN, George (Weyside Healers): Private healing by appointment.

Address: 15 Ardmore Avenue, Guildford, Surrey.
Tel: (0483) 39300

SOWTER, Irene Priscilla and Gerald Valentine: Principals, Universal Fellowship for Divine Healing. Contact and absent healing. Public demonstrations of healing given, not on demand but through spiritual guidance. Mrs Sowter gives clairvoyant, clairaudient or trance diagnosis. She is used as a medium for spirit operations to be performed.

Address: 18 Somers Road, Reigate, Surrey.
Tel: (07372) 42853

Sussex

BULL, Margaret (State Enrolled Nurse), NFSH Member. Contact and absent healing. This healer also has the gift of automatic writing.

Address: 25 The Poplars, Horsham, Sussex.
Tel: (0403) 54123

BURDITCH, Mrs Betsy: Contact and absent healing. Also healing via telephone consultation.

Address: 6 Berriedale Avenue, Hove, Sussex.
Tel: (0273) 776188

DOCTORS, Mrs Leah: Contact and absent healing. This healer also performs spirit operations. *The Healing Power* by B J Hatton, published in 1975, is the story of Mrs Doctors and her spirit guide Doctor Chang. Mrs Doctors was filmed at work for a *Whicker's World* television programme.

Address: 47 Goldstone Villas, Hove, Sussex.
Tel: (0273) 737746

West Midlands

THE BARRON HOWARD HEALING CENTRE (Members NFSH): Personal consultations. Two healers are normally in attendance. In addition to the two resident healers, there is also a visiting acupuncturist and osteopath, who is a member of the British Acupuncture Association. Leaflet sent on request.

Address: The Barron Howard Healing Centre, 48 High Street, Sutton Coldfield, West Midlands.
Tel: (021) 354 7893 or (021) 378 0214

VALANCE, Howard: Contact and absent healing.

Address: 68 Honeyborne Road, Sutton Coldfield, West Midlands.
Tel: (021) 378 1871

Wiltshire

WILLIAMS, Leslie Clifford: Magnetic healing and osteopathy. Contact and absent healing. Private consultations by appointment only.

Address: Pear Tree Cottage, Crudwell, Malmesbury, Wiltshire.
Tel: (06667) 314

Yorkshire

HOLLAND, Mrs Mary Selina: Some private healing but mostly absent healing and church healing. Mrs Holland is also a clairvoyant medium.

Address: 38 Glendale Drive, Harbour Road, Wibsey, Bradford, West Yorkshire.
Tel: (0274) 679827

ORUYE, Odie: Contact and absent healing plus travel. Odie Oruye is at present the Secretary of Bankfoot National Spiritualist Church, Bradford.

Address: 25 Archibald Street, Bradford, West Yorkshire.
Tel: (0274) 391798

Wales

BUXTON, Paul (SRN), Anita (SEN) and Gwyneth: Contact and absent healing. Members of this healing group will visit on request. Their work is voluntary; no fees are necessary.

Address: 5 Sunnybank, Fellows Lane, Caergwrle, Wrexham, Clwyd.

SPRINGALL, Mr and Mrs Beryl and Ernest: Provide a local contact and absent healing service, which is free of charge. For details of private or absent healing, please telephone or write.

Address: Elan Nant, Holway Road, Holywell, Clwyd, North Wales.
Tel: (0352) 713797

Eire

DORAN, John: Healing, both private consultations and absent healing. Personal healing takes place every Monday, Wednesday, Friday, Saturday and Sunday, between 1pm and 8pm. John Doran, psychic healer, is the seventh son of a seventh son. He also classes himself as a faith healer.

Address: Avalon, Barton Street, Tinahely, Co. Wicklow, Eire.

Healers

Healers are listed alphabetically below, either in the category of contact healer or absent healer. In many cases, you will find that a healer is listed under both classifications. Their city or county location is indicated alongside in brackets.

Readers are advised to study each healer's profile for further information.

Contact Healing

Abbott, Myra (see *Mediums*: Yorkshire)
Anderson, Keith (see *Mediums*: Avon)
Aqua (See *Mediums*: Surrey)
Augustus, John (see *Mediums*: London)
Baker, Joyce (Cornwall)
Barham, Irene (see *Mediums*: London)
Barron Howard Healing Centre, The (West Midlands)
Bourne, Brian (see *Mediums*: London)
Brace, Louise (see *Mediums*: London)
Brady, Julia (see *Mediums*: London)
Bridgford, Barbara (see *Mediums*: Yorkshire)
Brough-Eley, Leslie (see *Mediums*: London)
Bull, Margaret (Sussex)
Burnard, Barbara (Devon)
Buxton, Paul and Anita (Clwyd, Wales)
Carter, Maria-Diana (Somerset)
Cephas, Peter (see *Mediums*: Bedfordshire)
Cohen, Harold (see *Mediums*: Essex)
Coney, John (Norfolk)
Coombs, Martin (London)
Crane, Pamela and Gerard (see *Mediums*: Kent)

Crystal-Broadwood, Sylvia (London)
Dann-Szulc, Eileen (Middlesex)
Dixon, Ron and Frances (see *Mediums*: Kent)
Doctors, Leah (Sussex)
Doran, John (Co. Wicklow, Eire)
Durnin, Jackie (see *Mediums*: London)
Edwin, E (see *Mediums*: Mid-Glamorgan, Wales)
Everett, Lee (see *Mediums*: London)
Fordham, Roy (London)
Foster, Margaret (Newport, Isle of Wight)
Gainey (see *Mediums*: London)
Garman, Joan (see *Mediums*: London)
Ghani, M A (see *Mediums*: London)
Gibbard, Mike (see *Mediums*: Norfolk)
Hadleigh Healing Society (Suffolk)
Harlequin, The (see *Mediums*: London)
Holland, Mary Selina (Yorkshire)
Homewood, Elizabeth (Surrey)
Horner, Irene (Devon)
Jackson, Wendy (see *Mediums*: London)
James, Carol (see *Mediums*: Devon)
James, Ernie (see *Mediums*: London)
Jenkins, Janine and John (Port St Mary, Isle of Man)
Kiera (see *Mediums*: Kent)
Leech-Schwertzel, Madame (London)
Lena (see *Mediums*: London)
Lester, Aislinn (see *Mediums*: London)
Locke, Claudia (see *Mediums*: Dyfed, Wales)
Mamdani, Salim (see *Mediums*: London)
Mattman, Frederick (see *Mediums*: Kent)
Mattman, Pat (Kent)
Muriel (see *Mediums*: London)
Mussell, Derek (London)
New Barnet Healers (Hertfordshire)
Nicholas, Brian (see *Mediums*: Staffordshire)
Nock, Frederick (Hampshire)
Odie, Oruye (Yorkshire)
Old Ring of Bells Healing Sanctuary (Somerset)
Opfer, Duskrainer and Albert (Suffolk)

Pandya, Ashwin (see *Mediums*: London)
Pearse, Lilian (see *Mediums*: London)
Peplow, Patricia (see *Mediums*: London)
Player, Kathryn (see *Mediums*: London)
Plumley, Mr and Mrs (Somerset)
Potts, Owen (see *Mediums*: London)
Pullen, George (Surrey)
Rae, Margaret (see *Mediums*: London)
Ralston, Jenny (see *Mediums*: Sussex)
Reeve, Christopher (Lincolnshire)
Reeves, Sheila (see *Mediums*: Lancashire)
Scott, Harry (London)
Shirl (see *Mediums*: Essex)
Sowter, Irene and Gerald (Surrey)
Springall, Mr and Mrs (Clwyd, Wales)
Stalley, Edwin (London)
Stalley, Ena (London)
Tingey, Michael (London)
Truscott, La Verne (see *Mediums*: Cornwall)
Valance, Howard (West Midlands)
Wade, Myrna (see *Mediums*: Northumberland)
Wheatley, Ron (see *Mediums*: Kent)
Williams, Leslie (Wiltshire)
Winter, Rosemary (see *Mediums*: Surrey)
Wright, Ronald (Hertfordshire)
Wyndham, Phil and Kath (Devon)

Absent Healing

Baker, Joyce (Cornwall)
Bull, Margaret (Sussex)
Burditch, Mary (Sussex)
Burnard, Barbara (Devon)
Buxton, Paul and Anita (Clwyd, Wales)
Carter, Maria-Diana (Somerset)
Coney, John (Norfolk)
Coombs, Martin (London)
Crane, Pamela and Gerard (see *Mediums*: Kent)
Crystal-Broadwood, Sylvia (London)

Dabrowa, Betty (see *Mediums*: London)
Doctors, Leah (Sussex)
Doran, John (Co Wicklow, Eire)
Edwin, E (see *Mediums*: Mid-Glamorgan, Wales)
Fordham, Roy (London)
Foster, Margaret (Newport, Isle of Wight)
Gibbard, Mike (see *Mediums*: Norfolk)
Hadleigh Healing Society (Suffolk)
Holland, Mary Selina (Yorkshire)
Horner, Irene (Devon)
Jenkins, Janine and John (Port St Mary, Isle of Man)
King, Eve (Devon)
Lester, Aislinn (see *Mediums*: London)
Mattman, Pat (Kent)
New Barnet Healers (Hertfordshire)
Nock, Frederick (Hampshire)
Odie, Oruye (Yorkshire)
Old Ring of Bells Healing Sanctuary (Somerset)
Opfer, Duskrainer and Albert (Suffolk)
Player, Kathryn (see *Mediums*: London)
Purvis, Janis (see *Mediums*: Northumberland)
Reeve, Christopher (Lincolnshire)
Scott, Harry (London)
Sowter, Irene and Gerald (Surrey)
Springall, Mr and Mrs (Clwyd, Wales)
Stalley, Edwin (London)
Stalley, Ena (London)
Tingey, Michael (London)
Valance, Howard (West Midlands)
Williams, Leslie (Wiltshire)
Wright, Ronald (Hertfordshire)
Wyndham, Phil and Kath (Devon)

Guidelines

1. Please observe the courtesy of a stamped and self-addressed envelope for all correspondence that requires a reply.
2. Enquire about the type of consultation, fee and duration of reading, at the time that you enquire about an appointment. This will avoid any misunderstanding at a later date.
3. Do not call on a consultant without an appointment unless you have an arrangement to make informal visits.
4. Always make a note of the time and date of your appointment – never trust to memory.
5. Never arrive late for an appointment.
6. Always advise a consultant if you are unable to keep an appointment.
7. Many mediums and psychics visit homes by appointment, so you may find it convenient to have a home consultation if you are housebound. Home consultations are indicated in a consultant's profile by the word 'travel'.
8. Ask beforehand if you wish to take notes during a consultation, but do not be surprised if a consultant prohibits note-taking, for this can prove to be a distraction to concentration.
9. Mediums and psychics have a primary objective of helping people with problems; many of these people will be depressed because of their problems, but there are those who suffer from depression or mental illness who should under no circumstances suddenly make appointments to see consultants. Such an action could seriously aggravate a sensitive psychological condition.

Any responsible psychic will issue the same advice and there are very few exceptions to the rule.

Glossary

Astrology: A study and interpretation of the influence of the stars on human character, behaviour and destiny.

Cartomancy: A system of divination using either the Tarot or standard playing cards.

Clairaudience: The psychic ability to hear that which is not heard with the physical sense of sound.

Clairsentience: The strong intuitive sensing of an event or situation.

Clairvoyance: The psychic ability to see that which is not seen with the physical sense of sight.

Crystal: Glass or acrylic sphere which is used as a focal point to induce clairvoyance, or as a central point of concentration.

I-Ching: *The Book of Changes*. A traditional book of divination using a system of sixty-four hexagrams, through which the reciprocal play of Yin and Yang (male and female) is reflected. A timeless method of interpretation.

Numerology: An interpretation of the significance of numbers and combinations of numbers.

Palmistry: A system of interpretation by which the lines and characteristics of the palm are read.

Psychometry: Receiving psychic impressions via direct touch with an object. The object is quite often a personal item such as jewellery or a handwritten letter.

Runes: Symbols/letters of early North European origin. The runes have an occult tradition, making them a favoured choice of interpretation by some psychics.

Tarot: A total of seventy-eight cards consisting of a series of twenty-two cards and a set of fifty-six cards. These pictorial cards come from an early occult tradition.

6

Churches: The Spiritualists' National Union

History and Objects

The Spiritualists' National Federation was founded in July, 1890, at the instance of Mrs Emma Hardinge Britten, by a number of prominent Spiritualists in Manchester. At first the Federation was little more than a movable annual conference at which delegates from Spiritualist societies and individual Spiritualists could discuss problems of common interest. As a result of these conferences it became clear that the field of co-operation could be widened if the Federation obtained the legal status of a corporation which could hold real property.

In October 1901 the Spiritualists' National Union Limited was accordingly incorporated under the Companies Acts as a company limited by guarantee and in July 1902 it took over the assets, rights and obligations of the Federation.

Membership of the Union is open to individual Spiritualists as well as to churches and kindred bodies. Its primary object is to promote the advancement and diffusion of the religion and religious philosophy of Spiritualism on the basis of the Seven Principles:

1. The Fatherhood of God.
2. The Brotherhood of Man.
3. The Communion of Spirits and the Ministry of Angels.
4. The continuous existence of the human soul.
5. Personal responsibility.

6. Compensation and retribution hereafter for all the good and evil deeds done on earth.
7. Eternal progress open to every human soul.

It aims to unite Spiritualist Churches into a Spiritualist brotherhood and to secure for them full recognition as religious bodies.

Other objects specified in the Memorandum of Association include the encouragement of Spiritualist research, the certification of lecturers, exponents and teachers, the publication of Spiritualist literature and the promotion of mission work. The Union has taken a leading part in the foundation of the International Spiritualist Federation, which unites Spiritualists of many countries.

In 1948 the British Spiritualists' Lyceum Union (which had been founded in 1890) amalgamated with the Spiritualists' National Union and its work for the spiritual education of children and young people has been carried on as part of the regular work of the Union.

The policy of the Union is formulated by a democratically elected Council and its implementation and the direction of the affairs of the Union are administered by a National Executive Committee through a number of Committees. The most important of these are the Trust Property, Education and Publications, Exponents and Public Relations, General Purposes and Arthur Findlay College Committees. Local affairs are delegated to fourteen district councils, the executive committees of which are directly elected by the members of the district councils themselves.

Spiritualist Churches do not have resident ministers or pastors. They are served by different exponents from week to week and the Union does not interfere with their discretion and autonomy in such matters. The Union has, however, compiled a register of recognized exponents and from these has selected a number for appointment as National Spiritualist Ministers.

Churches Listed by District and Area

East London and District Area

(Abbreviations: KB = Kindred Body. AB = Associated Body.)

Balham – Hamilton Hall, 211 High Road, Balham, SW17.

Morden (Branch of Balham SS) – 214 Morden Road, Merton, SW19.

Barkingside – IRDSA Hall, Craven Gardens, Fulwell Cross.

Battersea – Bennerley Hall, 46 Bennerley Road, Northcote Road, SW11. (Near Clapham Junction.)

Billericay – Labour Rooms, 21 High Street.

Brentwood SC – Primrose Hill, Brentwood, Essex.

Brixton – St Michael's Road, Stockwell, SW9.

Bury St Edmunds and District – Friends Meeting House, St John's Street, Bury St Edmunds, Suffolk.

Cambridge – Myers' Memorial Hall, Thompson's Lane.

Canterbury – 8a Kirby's Lane.

Cheshunt – The Chapel, Bishop's College, Churchgate, Cheshunt.

Clapham – 11a North Street, Old Town, SW4.

Colchester – Fennings Chase, Priory Street.

Croydon – Chatsworth Road.

Dartford CSC – 15 Tower Road.

Edmonton – 14 Linnell Road, N18.

Eltham – 64 Well Hall Road, SW9.

Enfield – Beacon of Light CSC, 331 Carterhatch Lane, Forty Hill.

Felixstowe CSC – Guide Hut, Garrison Lane.

Gillingham (Kent) – 177 Canterbury Street.

Gravesend – 19 Clarence Place.

Hastings – Spiritualist Brotherhood Church, 8/9 Portland Place.

Hoddesdon Spiritualist Fellowship – Friends Hall, Lord Street, Hoddesdon.

Horley Spiritualist Centre – Strawson Hall, Albert Road.

Ilford – 270/273 High Road.

AB Ipswich Psy. Society – the Cedars, Anglesey Road.

KB Kent Psychic Groups – 7 Alma Road, Herne Bay.

Kingston – Villiers Road, Kingston-on-Thames.

Laindon – Temple of Light, Bedford Road.

Little Ilford CSC – Third Avenue, Manor Park, E12.

Lowestoft – 13 Gordon Road.

Manor Park – Shrewsbury Road, Forest Gate, E7.

New Malden – Park Road.

North London – 425 Hornsey Road, N19.

Norwich – Chapel Field Road.

Palmer's Green – Temple of the Trinity, 95 Green Lanes, Palmer's Green, N13.

Plaistow – 161 Cumberland Road, E13.

Rochester Square, Rochester Square, Camden Road, NW1.

Sevenoaks – Toc H Room, 12b High Street.

Sutton – St Barnabas Road.

Tolworth – 156 Ewell Road, Surbiton.

Tunbridge Wells – 33 Queens Road, Tunbridge Wells, Kent.

Walthamstow – Vestry Road, E17.

Walthamstow – Lyceum Church, 39 Coleridge Road, off Palmerston Road, E17.

Wandsworth CSC – Waldron Hall, 524 Garrett Lane, SW17.

Welwyn Garden City CSC – Marsden Green, Handside Lane.

Westcliff – Hildaville Drive.

West Norwood – Ullswater Road, West Norwood, SE27.

West Wickham – Surrey Road, off High Street.

Wickham Lane SNC – 95 Wickham Lane, Plumstead, SE2.

Woodford – 9 Grove Crescent, South Woodford.
AB Wood Green – High Road, corner of Maryland Road, N22.

West London and District Area

Acton – The Cottage, Woodhurst Road, Acton, W3.

Aylesbury – Mount Street. (Near railway station.)

Bedford CSC – 21 Ashburnham Road, Bedford.

Bognor Regis – 7 Sudley Road, Bognor Regis.

Brighton – Edward Street.

Brighton and Hove Central S.C. – 9/10 Boundary Passage, Brighton.

Burnt Oak – Watling Centre, 145 Orange Hill Road.

Camberley – 112 Gordon Road, Camberley.

Crawley CSC – Capel Lane, Gossops Green.

Ealing – 66/68 Uxbridge Road, Ealing, W13.

Feltham Spiritual Centre – Labour Hall, Manor Place, Bedfort Lane, Feltham.

Fleet and District – 193 Aldershot Road (Crookham Crossroad), Church Crookham.

Fulham – Kelvedon Road.

Guildford and District – Guildford Institute, Ward Street.

Hampton Hill – 12 Windhill Road.

Harrow – Vaughan Road, Harrow.

Hayes – Albert Hall, Albert Road.

Hitchin – Whinbush Road.

Hounslow – Sp. Mission, 97a Hanworth Road. (Corner Douglas Road.)

Hounslow SNC – 656 London Road.

Huntingdon SNC – Castle Moat Road.

Ickenham – Windmill Hall, Pembroke Road, Ruislip, Middlesex.

Kenton SNC – 35 Churchill Avenue, Kenton.

Kettering – St Peter's Avenue.

Lancing – Women's Institute Hall, Robert Road, Lancing, Sussex.

Letchworth – Vasanta Hall, Gernon Walk, Letchworth.

Littlehampton and Rustington – Rustington Village Hall, Woodlands Avenue, Rustington, Sussex.

Luton – 20 Cardiff Grove, Luton.

Maidenhead SNC – York Road, Maidenhead, Berkshire.

Milton Keynes – New Bradwell Community Centre, New Bradwell.   Communications c/o 83 Newport Road.

Newbury – Liberal Hall, Bartholomew Street.

Oxford – 39b Oxford Road, Cowley, Oxford.

Rayners Lane, 359b Rayners Lane, Pinner, Middlesex.

Reading – 'York Lodge', 81 Baker Street.

Richmond – 97 Church Road and Ormond Road.

Slough – Red Cross Hall, 1 Osbourne Road, Slough.

Southall – Hortus Road, The Green, Southall, Middlesex.

St Albans – 40 Granville Road.

Stevenage – Bedwell Community Centre, Bedwell Crescent.

Walton-on-Thames – Halfway, Hersham Road.

Wembley – 10/12 St John's Road.

Wimbledon – 136 Hartfield Road, SW19.

Windsor – Adelaide Square, King's Road.

Woking and District – 'Waltham', Grove Road.

Unattached Church

Brighton – Brotherhood Gate, 21c St James Street.

East Midlands District

Belper – New Road.

Brimington – John Street.

Burton on Trent – Horninglow SC, Farm Road, Horninglow.

Chesterfield – Baden Powell Road.

Clay Cross – Bridge Street.

Coalville – Bridge Street.

Derby Central – Rear of 2 Forester Street.

Derby – Charnwood Street.

Eastwood – Edward Road.

Grantham – 13a Elmer Street.

Kirkby-in-Ashfield – Low Moor Road.

Leicester – 115 Vaughan Way.

Leicester Progressive – St James' Street, Humberstone Gate.

Long Eaton – Broad Street. (Near library.)

Loughborough CSC – Steeple Row. (Off Rectory Place.)

Mansfield – Dallas Street.

Newark – 8 Albert Street. (Near Beumond Close.)

Nottingham – 1st National Spiritualist Church, 123 Derby Road.

Nottingham – 1a Beaconsfield Street, Hyson Green.

Nottingham – Nottingham SC and 1st Prog. Lyceum, Cavendish Hall, Hall Street, Sherwood.

Peterborough – 29 Silverwood Road.

Ripley and District – Argyll Road, Ripley.

Sleaford – 100 Westgate.

Sutton-in-Ashfield – The Twitchell.

West Midlands District

Birmingham – The Digbeth Civic Hall, Digbeth.

Birmingham 'Forward' – Earlsbury Gardens.

Birmingham – King's Heath, 5 Springfield Road.

Birmingham – Lozells, Church Hall, rear of 30 John Street, Lozells, Birmingham.

Bloxwich – Revival Street.

Bromsgrove – Co-op Chambers, High Street. Enquiries to: Mrs P Stocks, The Bower, Far Forest, Near Kidderminster, Worcestershire.

Brownhills Excelsior – High Street, Brownhills, Walsall, Staffordshire.

Brownhills Temple of Light – High Street, Brownhills, Walsall, Staffordshire.

Burslem – 66 Moorland Road.

Coventry Broadgate – 73/83 Eagle Street, Foleshill, Coventry.

Coventry Parkside – Parkside (back of Ringway St John), Coventry.

Darlaston – Pinfold Street Exhibition.

Evesham – Unitarian School Room, Oak Street.
Fenton – 60/62 King Street, Stoke-on-Trent.
Hanley – Town Road, Stoke-on-Trent.
Hinckley – Station Road.
Leamington Spa – 1/2 Holly Street, Leamington Spa.
Longton – Lightwood Road, Stoke-on-Trent.
Newtown – Meeting Rooms, Matchborough West, Redditch, Worcestershire.
Northampton – 89 St Michael's Road.
Nuneaton – Norman Avenue.
Oldbury – Canal Street.
Redditch – c/o Redditch Carnivall Headquarters, Hewell Road.
Rugby – Pennington Street.
Smethwick – Thimblemill Road, Bearwood, Smethwick.
Solihull – Society of Spiritualists, Manor House, High Street, Solihull.
Stourbridge – Union Street. (Three minutes from bus terminal.)
Stratford-on-Avon – Masonic Hall, Great William Street.
Sutton Coldfield – Kenelm Road. (Off Manor Hill.)
Tamworth – Victoria Road/Marmion Street.
Telford 1st – St James Hall, Stirchley Village, Telford, Shropshire.
Tunstall – 1 Piccadilly Street.
Walsall – Vicarage Place. Enquiries to: Mrs E Holliday, 25 Woodside Way, Aldridge, Walsall, West Midlands.
Wellington – Regent Street, Wellington, Telford, Salop.
Wolverhampton – Waterloo Road.

Northern District

Ashington – 9 Laburnham Terrace.
Beamish Temple – Roseberry Gardens, Beamish.
Bedlington – Back Ravensworth Street, Bedlington Station.
Benwell – 40 Adelaide Terrace.
Billingham – Chapel Road.
Birtley – Mitchell Street.
Blackhill – Park Road.

Blyth Progressive – 36 Bowes Street.
Chester-le-Street – 2 Ashley Terrace.
Choppington – Church Avenue, Scotland Gate.
Craghead – Front Street.
Darlington – 181 Northgate
Dunston – Ellison Road. (Near Dun Cow Inn.)
Durham City – John Street.
Easington Lane – Derwent Street.
Eldon Lane – Front Street.
Felling – Crowhall Lane (Community Centre), Felling Square.
Gateshead – Eden Prog. SC, Rectory Hall, St Cuthberts Place, Bensham.
Gateshead – 35 Gladstone Terrace West.
Grangetown (Middlesborough) – Pochin Road.
Hirst – Milburn Road, Ashington.
Horden – East Coast Road.
Jarrow – Shopping Precinct.
Middlesbrough – 115 Borough Road.
Monkwearmouth – Newcastle Road.
Newburn-on-Tyne – New Community Centre. (Near Boyd Street.)
Newcastle-on-Tyne – Spiritual Evidence Society, 11 Osborne Road, Jesmond.
Newcastle Heaton and Byker – Tosson Terrace, Heaton.
North Shields – Rippon Hall, 42 Stanley Street West, Tyne and Wear.
Philadelphia – Enquiries to: W. Christie, 2 The Cottages, Low Lambton, New Penshaw, Tyne and Wear.
Redcar – Red Cross Hall, Pierson Street.
Saltburn – Community Centre, Windsor Road.
Seaham – Cornelia Terrace, Marlborough, Seaham.
Seaton Delaval – Station Road. (Next to Ivanhoe Forge.)
Shildon – Newlands Avenue, Middleton Road.
South Shields – 33 Beach Road.
Spennymoor – Stratton Street.
Sunderland – 1 Grange Terrace.
Wallsend-on-Tyne – Park Road.
West Stanley – Belle Street.

Whickham – Community Centre, Front Street, Whickham.

Whitley Bay – 10 South Parade.

Willington – Chapel Street.

Manchester District

Altrincham – Clarendon Avenue, Stockport Road, Altrincham.

Ashton-under-Lyne – Burlington Street.

Bolton – Bradford Street.

Bury – Russell Street, Bury.

Buxton – Holker Road.

Collyhurst – Paget Street.

Congleton – Park Road.

Crewe – Adelaide Street, Crewe, Cheshire.

Dearnley – New Road, Dearnley, near Littleborough, Lancashire.

Denton – Annan Street, near Crown Point.

Dukinfield – Astley Street.

Hadfield – Jones Street.

Horwich – Chorley New Road.

Hyde – Great Norbury Street.

Little Hulton – Community Centre, Eastham Way.

Longsight – Daisy Bank Road, Victoria Park, Manchester.

Macclesfield – Cumberland Street.

Manchester – 151 Raby Street. (Corner of Moss Lane East.)

Manchester Healing Centre – Milton Hall, Deansgate.

Middleton – 39 Gilmour Street.

Moston – 150 Church Lane, Moston, Manchester.

Northwich – 16a Hadfield Street. (Off Station Road.)

Oldham – 157–9 Ashton Road.

Saddleworth – 161 High Street, Uppermill, near Oldham.

Salford – Cross Lane, Liverpool Street.

Shaw – Duke Street. (Off Beal Lane.)

South Manchester – 2 Alexandra Road South, Whalley Range, Manchester.

St Helens – Charles Street.

Stockport SNC and Lyceum – 82 Chatham Street, Edgeley.
Whitefield – Victoria Lane, Whitefield M/C.
Woodhouse Park – The Social Centre, Bromley Road, Wythenshawe.

Unattached Church

Cheetham Hill – Halliwell Lane.

North Lancashire and Cumbria District

Bacup – 15 Yorkshire Street, Todmorden Road.
Barnoldswick – Central Progressive, Saint James Road. (Opposite Parish Church.)
Barrow-in-Furness – Psychological Hall, Dalkeith Street.
Barrow-in-Furness – Saint John's Ambulance Rooms (temporary address).
Blackburn – Saint Peter Street.
Blackpool – 71 Albert Road, Central.
Burnley – Hammerton Street.
Cleveleys – 8 Cleveleys Avenue.
Clitheroe – Greenacre Street.
Colne – Spring Lane.
Darwen – Victoria Street.
Fleetwood – Oak Street.
Great Harwood – Clayton Street, Great Harwood.
Lancaster – Britten Hall, Bulk Road.
Lancaster – Alliance, Moor Lane (Methodist School Room), Lancaster.
Millom – 25a Holborn Hill.
Morecambe – Temple of Light United, West End Road, Morecambe.
Preston – Ethical, Moor Lane. (Across from Telephone House.)
Rawtenstall – Back of Ormerod Street.
Saint Annes – Pensioners' Hall, Saint Alban's Road, Saint Annes-on-the-Sea.

Unattached Church

Kendal – Beacon of Light, Beacon Building, Stramongate, Kendal.

South-west Lancashire and Cheshire District

Allerton – Sp. Assoc., Dudley Hall, Blenheim Road, Liverpool.
Birkenhead – Mount Grove.
Chester First – Common Hall Street. (Off Bridge Street.)
Colwyn Bay – 17 Woodland Road West. (Near Public Library.)
Leigh Temple – 3 Evans Street.
Liverpool – 14 Daulby Street.
Rhyl CSC – Grynfa Villa, off Thorpe Street.
Rock Ferry – 130 Bedford Road.
Runcorn – Ashridge Street.
Southport – Hawkshead Street.
Wallasey – 61 Withens Lane.
Wallasey Village – 237 Wallasey Village.
Warrington – 66 Academy Street.
Waterloo (Liverpool) – 28 South Road.
Widnes – Lacey Street.
Wigan – Crompton Road.

Scottish District

Aberdeen – Bon Accord Spiritualist Church, 41 Loch Street, (Off George Street), Aberdeen.
Aberdeen – Psychic Centre and Healing Sanctuary, 71 Dee Street, Aberdeen.
Alloa CSC – Town Hall, Marshill, Alloa.
Ayr – Church of Psychic Science, 10 Alloway Place (ground floor flat), The Fort, Ayr.
Belfast – 134 Malone Avenue, Belfast 9.
Dumfries – The Day Centre, George Street.
Dundee – Progressive, 31 Benvie Road.

Dundee – Church of the Spirit, 142 Nethergate.
Dunfermline – 3 Lady Campbell's Walk.
KB Edinburgh – 34 Albany Street.
Edinburgh Gayfield – 246 Morrison Street.
Falkirk and District Church – 8 Burnhead Lane.
Glasgow – Association of Spiritualists, 6/7 Somerset Place.
Glasgow – Central Association of Spiritualists, 64 Berkeley Street.
Hamilton – Park Road.
Kilmarnock – 28/30 Old Mill Road.
Langside and District – Langside Hall, Langside Avenue.
Livingston – Craigs Park Pavilion, Craigshill, Livingston.
Lochgelly – 37/39 Bank Street.
Paisley – Scots Girls' Friendly Society Home Hall, off New Street.
Pathead and Dysart – Commercial Street, Kirkcaldy.
Perth – 40 New Row.
Portobello – 20a Bath Street, Edinburgh 15.
Stirling – 27 King Street.

Southern District

Andover Spiritual Fellowship – Moore Hall, Church Close, Newbury Street.
Basingstoke – 28 Victoria Road.
Bournemouth – 16 Bath Road.
Chichester – SNC and Healing Centre, Friends Meeting House, Prior Road.
Christchurch – 196b Barrack Road.
Cowes – Newport Road, Cowes, Isle of Wight.
Eastleigh – Corner Grantham and Southampton Roads.
Gosport – 183 Forton Road.
Havant and District – Homewell House, 22 Homewell, Havant.
Hayling Island – Conservative Hall, 31 Elm Grove, Menge Ham, Hayling Island.
Hythe – West Shore House, West Street, Hythe, Southampton.
Parkstone – 17 Victoria Road.

Porchester and Fareham – Red Cross Hut, Lower Quay, Fareham, Hants.

Portsmouth Progressive – Vivash Road, Fratton, Portsmouth.

Portsmouth Temple of Spiritualism – 73a Victoria Road South, Southsea.

Ryde, Isle of Wight – Corner Belvedere Street and Park Road.

Salisbury – Sp. Meeting House, 22 Bedwin Street.

Salisbury – Silver Birch Sanctuary, 9 Hadrians Close, Lower Road, Bemerton.

Southampton, Bitterne and District – Top of Lance's Hill, Bitterne Road, Bitterne, Southampton.

Southampton, Cavendish Grove – The Avenue.

Southampton/Shirley – 10 Grove Road.

Southampton/Swaythling – Portswood Road. (Sirdar Road bus stop)

Southampton Woolston Sanctuary of Peace – 'Eastcliffe', Portsmouth Road, Woolston. (Near Library.)

Totton – Nursury School, Testwood Lane, Totton.

Ventnor, Isle of Wight – 8 Victoria Street.

Wilton – 3 Warminster Avenue.

South-Western District

Bath First – Manvers Place, 16 Old Orchard Street.

Bath (Beacon of Light) – 10 Laura Place.

Bideford – Spiritualist Church, Hart Street.

Bridgwater – Moose Hall, Green Dragon Lane.

Bristol Aquarian Sp. Society – Hillfields Park Community Centre, Thicket Avenue, Hillfields, Bristol.

Bristol Bedminster and Bedminster Down Temple of Truth – Hebron Road, Bedminster.

Bristol Brislington – Saint John's Hall, Wick Road, Brislington 4.

Bristol (Filton) – Co-op Hall, Northville, Filton.

Bristol First – Surrey House, 10 Surrey Street, Saint Paul's.

Bristol (Knowle Spiritualist Foundation) – Co-op Hall, Greenmore Road.

Bristol (Redland) – 31 Belmont Road, Saint Andrews.

Bristol (Sacred Trust) – 70 Hampton road, Redland. (Side entrance.)

Bristol (Westbury Park) – Cairns Road, Westbury Park.

Bristol Universal – Bishop Street, Bristol.

Cheltenham – Bennington Street.

Chippenham – Coopers Hall, Market Place.

Clevedon – Red Cross Hall, Old Street.

Devonport (Brunswick) – Keppel Place, Stoke, Devonport.

Exeter – York Road. Enquiries: Mrs W E Gillard, 1 Crabb Lane, Alphington, Exeter.

Gloucester – 2a Brunswick Square.

Liskeard and District – Long Room Public Hall, West Street, Liskeard.

Melksham – King Street, Melksham, Wiltshire.

Newton Abbot – East Street. (Next to General Hospital.)

Okehampton – Committee Room, Conservative Club, Mill Road.

Paignton – Manor Corner, Preston, Paignton.

Plymouth Grimstone – 39 Houndiscombe Road, Plymouth.

Plymouth (Hillsborough) – Connaught Avenue, Mutley.

Swindon – Spiritualist Church and Healing Sanctuary, 31 Devizes Road, Swindon, Wiltshire.

Taunton – Chestnut Tree, Cannon Street, Car Park.

Wadebridge – The Town Hall, The Platt.

Wells Spiritualists' Guild – Saint John's Ambulance Hut, Princes Road, Wells.

Weston-Super-Mare – Blue Cross CSC., Tivoli Lane, Boulevard.

Weston-Super-Mare – First National, Stafford Road.

Yeovil First – Unitarian Hall, Goldcroft, Yeovil.

South Wales District

Aberavon and Port Talbot – 1 Tydraw Place.
Aberkenfig – Pandy Square.
Barry First – Buttrills Road.
Blackwood – 204 High Street.
Bridgend – The Rhiw.
Caerau – 3 Fowlers Place.
Cardiff First – 1 Park Grove.
AB First Cardiganshire – Memorial Hall, Aberaeron, Dyfed.
Cwm and District – River View.
Ferndale – 1 Fountain Street.
Gwaun-cae-Gurwen – Neuadd Road.
Markham – 74 Bryn Road.
Merthyr Tydfil – Temple, Tramroadside North.
Merthyr Tydfil – Saint Margaret's, Garth Place.
Neath – Saint John's, Windsor Buildings, The Ropewalk.
Newport – 29 Charles Street.
Pembroke Dock – 43 Queen Street.
Penarth – Red Cross Hall, Woodland Place.
Pontygwaith – Saint Margaret's, 86 Llewellyn Street.
Port – 11a Pontypridd Road.
Treforest – Cwrch y Gwas Road, off Broadway, Pontypridd.
Treherbert (Rhondda Progressive) – Dumfries Street.
Troedyrhiw – Saint David's Wyndham Street.
Ystalyfera – Ysgol Gyfun, Saint David's Road.

Yorkshire: Bradford District

Benkfoot – Bowling Old Lane.
Batley – 457 Bradford Road. (Below bus station.)
Batley Carr – Carr Street.
Brighouse – Martin Street.
Dewsbury – 14 Wellington Road.
Halifax – Bedford Street.
Harrogate – Burton Chambers, 21a Beulah Street.
Hebden Bridge – Hope Street.

Idle – 409 Highfield Road, Towngate.
Keighley – Heber Street.
Morley – Zoar Street. (Off Commercial Road.)
Saltaire – 7 Moorhead Lane, Shipley.
Skipton – Romille Street.
Sowerby Bridge – Hollins Lane.

Yorkshire: Leeds District

Armley – 1 Greenhill Road, Leeds 12.
Brierley – Church Street.
Castleford – Lower Oxford Street.
Grimsby – Duncombe Street.
Heckmondwike – Walkley Lane.
Hemsworth – Grove Lane.
Huddersfield – Old Leeds Road.
Hull – 20 Pearson Park.
Knaresborough – Knaresborough House, High Street.
New Clee – Enquiries: L Collins, 3 Jackson Street, Grimsby.
Normanton – 172/174 Castleford Road.
Ossett – Ventnor Way.
Otley – 38 Newmarket.
Quarmby – Harp Road, Longwood, Huddersfield.
Scarborough – 5 Queen Street.
South Elmsall – Church Street.
Wakefield – Peterson Road.
Warmsworth – Edlington Lane.
York – Spen Lane.

Unattached Church

Doncaster – College Road.

Barnsley – Pitt Street.
Barnsley – Hindle Street, off Racecommon Road.
Bentley – Rostholme Yard, off Askern Road, Bentley, Doncaster.
Doncaster – Catherine Street.
Mexborough – Bank Street.
Moorends – Marshland Road.
Parkgate – Ashwood Road, Parkgate.
Rotherham – Percy Street.
Sheffield Attercliffe – Bold Street.
Sheffield Darnall – 315 Shirland Lane.
Sheffield Centre – 1 Clarkson Street.
Sheffield Heeley Woodseats – 57 Club Garden Walk.
Sheffield Meersbrook – 109 Witham Road, Broomhill.
Stainforth – Station Road.
West Melton – 14 Barnsley Road.
Wombwell – Kelvin Grove.
Worksop – George Street.

All enquiries concerning The Spiritualists' National Union, should be addressed to: The Spiritualists' National Union, Britten House, Stansted Hall, Stansted, Essex. Telephone: (0279) 812705.

The Greater World Christian Spiritualist League and Association

Why Christian Spiritualism? There are Spiritualists who are not Christians, and there are Christians who repudiate Spiritualism. The disagreement of the orthodox Churches with what Christian Spiritualism seeks to teach is not easy to understand, when we consider the many instances of spirit communion that are recorded in the Old Testament, the encouragement to use spiritual gifts contained in the Epistles of St Paul, and the teachings and practice of Jesus Christ himself. It is a fact that the very basis of Christianity rests upon definite manifestations of spirit power.

The attitude of Spiritualists who are not Christian is somewhat different, apparently arising from the desire to break clean away from the old teachings of religion and substitute something entirely different – it is, in fact, a case of the 'swing of the pendulum'. At the extreme end of the swing are those who deny the very existence of God himself, claiming that Man is a god. In a small measure this is so, for within Man is that spark of the Divine that will, in time, find its freedom from the restrictions of the grosser body of flesh when physical death takes place.

There are those who accept the Fatherhood of God, and look to him with reverence and love, and yet they regard Christ merely as a medium of outstanding merit. The Christian Spiritualist, however, regards Christ as the only means by which we can know what God is like. Christ represents the accessible, understandable aspect of the Father that can be loved and whose example as Man, although representing an ideal, can be strived towards and emulated. Christian Spiritualism takes us back to the worship practised by the early Christians. We hail Christ as the 'Saviour' because his loving sacrifice, shown in his life rather than in his physical death, saved the world from descending into depths from which it could not emerge. We do not believe he bears our burden of wrong-doing for us – that falls upon ourselves, for even God himself cannot learn our lessons for us.

The Founding of the Greater World Movement

In 1921, a highly evolved being from the realms of Spirit manifested through the trance-mediumship of Miss Winifred Moyes. It was soon realized that this communicator, who called himself Zodiac, was able to give a teaching of great wisdom, and without any doubt was inspired by the love vibration of the Christ. The Zodiac Circle came into being, and the messages were taken down by a member of the Circle, Miss D Moyes, and reproduced in typewritten, and then duplicated, form. Gradually, the messages became known to hundreds of people, who received the Scripts by private circulation. By 1928 some 600 copies were mimeographed each week and distributed to readers, who passed them on to others.

The Scripts established themselves into a definite form of teaching, and through the continuous widening interest they aroused, *The Greater World* weekly paper was started for the sole purpose of spreading these wise teachings, for it was clear that Zodiac was engaged in a great spiritual Mission to Earth. The paper was founded at Easter, 1928, and now circulates in many countries. It is the only Christian Spiritualist paper in the world and is a teaching paper.

From these early beginnings the Greater World has grown into a worldwide movement.

The churches listed under the Greater World Christian Spiritualist League, which was formed in 1931, are affiliated to the movement by reason of their desire to worship God according to their light. Within the framework of the league they are autonomous, looking to the Greater World

Association for help and advice on matters of a material as well as a spiritual nature.

Mediums who receive the Greater World Certificate of Registration, and finally its Diploma, work within the framework of the Greater World Movement, having committed themselves to this ministry through their desire to serve Spiritualism under the leadership of Jesus Christ.

The nine Clauses of The Greater World Christian Spiritualist League

1. I believe in one God who is love.
2. I accept the leadership of Jesus Christ.
3. I believe that God manifests through the illimitable power of the Holy Spirit.
4. I believe in the survival of the human soul and its individuality after physical death.
5. I believe in the communion with God, with his angelic ministers, and with the souls functioning in conditions other than the earth life.
6. I believe that all forms of life created by God intermingle, are interdependent and evolve until perfection is attained.
7. I believe in the perfect justice of the divine laws governing all life.
8. I believe that sins committed can only be rectified by the sinner himself or herself, through the redemptive power of Jesus Christ, by repentance and service to others.
9. THE PLEDGE: I will at all times endeavour to be guided in my thoughts, words and deeds by the teaching and example of Jesus Christ.

Churches Listed by County, Area and Country

Avon

Bristol – Seymour CS Church and Nursing Home, 26 Sussex Place, Bristol 2.

Bedfordshire

Bedford – CS Fellowship, 21 Ashburnham Road.
Luton – CS Church, 47a Leagrave Road.

Buckinghamshire

High Wycombe – CS Church, Mount Pleasant Hall, Oxford Road.
Slough – Manor Park CS Church, Baylis House Annexe, Stoke Poges Lane.

Cambridgeshire

Peterborough – CS Church, Harris Street.
Wisbech – CS Church, Alexandra Road.

Cleveland

Middlesbrough – GWCS Church, 56 Gresham Road.
Norton CS Church, 26 Darlington Lane, Norton-on-Tees.

Cornwall

Falmouth – Central CS Church, 2 Quarry Hill.

Cumbria

Workington – Solway CS Church, Saint George's Hall, 4a Peter Street.

Derbyshire

Chesterfield – Saint Margaret's CS Church, Wheatbridge Road.
Swadlincote – CSC, Highfield Street.

Devonshire

Barnstaple – N. Devon S. Fellowship, Salem Hall, Higher Church Street.
Dawlish – SC, 16 Albert Street.
Ilfracombe – CS Church, Greenclose Road.
Plymouth – CS Crusader Fellowship and S Healing, 5 Oreston Road, Plymstock.
Teignmouth – CS Church, 14a Orchard Gardens.
Tiverton – CS Church, 'Riverside', Gold Street.

Dorset

Bournemouth – Silver Cross CS Church, 14 Maple Road, Winton, Bournemouth.
Poole – CS Church, 18 Kingland Road.
Weymouth – CS Healing Centre, Oddfellows Hall, 14 Market Street.

Essex

Billericay – CS Church, Labour Hall, 21 High Street.
Clacton-on-Sea – CS Church, 19 Oxford Road.
Colchester – CS Church, Labour Hall, Eld Lane.
Colchester – Temple of Light, 117 Shrub End Road.
Dovercourt – CS Church, 401 Main Road, Dovercourt, Harwich.

Leigh-on-Sea – Saint Cecilia CS Church, 9 Lord Roberts Avenue.

Thundersley – CS Church, 'Coombe Wood', Bread and Cheese Hill, London Road.

Hampshire

Alton – CS Church, Community Centre, Amery Street.

Basingstoke – CS Church, 75 Southern Road.

Winchester – CS Church, c/o The Winchester Centre, Parchment Street.

Hereford and Worcestershire

Kidderminster – CS Church, 16 Shubbery Street.

Hertfordshire

Barnet – Centre of Fellowship, 1a Union Street.

Letchworth – CS Church, Howard Hall, Norton Way.

Welwyn Garden City – CS Church, Marsden Green. (Off Handside Lane.)

Humberside

Bridlington – CS Church, 10 The Promenade. (Above Pearsons.)

Cleethorpes – Saint Peter's CS Church, Coronation Road.

Hull – Saint John's CS Church, 19 John Street.

Sudbury and District – CS Church, Village Hall, Bures Road, Great Cornard, Sudbury.

Kingston upon Hull – Sanctuary of the Spirit, 509 Hessle Road.

Kingston upon Hull – Temple of Truth, 178a Holderness Road.

Scunthorpe – CS Church, 25a Chapel Street.

Kent

Ashford – CS Church, Friends House, Albert Road.
Bexleyheath – CS Church, 85 Lion Road.
Broadstairs – CS Church, 8a Saint Peter's Road.
Dartford – CS Church, 15 Tower Road.
Dover – CS Church, Oddfellows Club, Pencester Road.
Folkestone – CS Church, Masonic Hall, 11 Grace Hill.
Gillingham – CS Church, 177 Canterbury Street.
Maidstone – CS Church, Tonbridge Road.
Orpington – Spiritual Progress Centre, Liberal Hall, Station Road.
Ramsgate – GWCS Church, Rear 23, Chilton Lane.
Sevenoaks – GWCS Centre, 65 Greatness Lane.
Sheerness – CS Society, Labour Hall, High Street.
Tonbridge – CS Church, YMCA, Shipbourne Road.

Lancashire

Blackpool – GWCS Church, 160 Lytham Road. (Near Broomfield.)
Morecambe – CS Church, Labour Hall, Battismore Road.
Preston – CS Church, Blue Bell Place, Church Street.

Leicestershire

Leicester – CS Sanctuary of Light, 73 London Road.
Loughborough – CS Church, Steeple Row.

Lincolnshire

Boston – CS Church and Healing Sanctuary, 123 High Street.
Lincoln – CS Church, 11 Portland Street.

Greater London

Ashford – CS Church, Community Centre, Chesterfield Road.

Clapham – CS Church, 1 Voltaire Road, SW4.

Ealing – Lileth Sanctuary of Healing, 12 Somerset Road, West Ealing, W13.

Eastcote – CS Church, Windmill Hall, Pembroke Road, Ruislip.

Enfield – Beacon of Light, 248 Carter Hatch Lane, Forty Hill.

Finchley – CS Church, Woodberry Hall, 4 Woodberry Grove, N12.

Holland Park – GW Sanctuary, 3 Lansdowne Road, W11.

Norbury – CS Healing Sanctuary, 47 Norbury Crescent, SW16.

Plumstead – CSC, RASC Hall, The Links, SW18.

Upminster – CS Church, 1a Belmont Avenue.

Wandsworth – CS Church, Waldron Hall, 524 Garratt Lane, SW17.

Wood Green – CS Church, 'Langford', High Road, N22. (Corner Maryland Road.)

West Norwood – CS Church, Ullswater Road, SW27.

Wimbledon – SC, 136 Hartfield Road, SW19.

Greater Manchester

Manchester – (Davyhulme) Saint Stephen's CS Church, 2a Lostock Road, Davyhulme, Urmston, Manchester.

Manchester – Stretford CS Church, Edge Lane, Stretford. (Opposite Railway Station.)

Manchester – Denbigh CS Church, Balleratt Street, Levenshulme.

Manchester – Winton CS Church, 70 New Lane, Winton, Eccles.

Stockport – CS Church, Old Road.

Stockport – GWCS Sanctuary, Walnut Tree Road, Cheadle Heath.

Merseyside

Liverpool – Psychic Truth Society, 44 Parkfield Road.

West Midlands

Bilston – Central CS Church, Broad Street.
Birmingham – Harborne Healing Centre, 144–146 Weoley Park Road, Weoley Castle.
Birmingham – Yardley, Saint Michael's Healing Sanctuary, Milton Crescent.
Birmingham – Selly Oak CS Church, Selly Oak Institute, Bristol Road.
Birmingham – Ward End CS Church, Church Walk, Wallbank Road, Washwood Heath.
Birmingham – Midland Soc. of Sp., 174 Edmund Street.
Coventry – CSC, Villiers Street.

Nottinghamshire

Mansfield – CS Church, 1a Southwell Road West.
Nottingham – Daybrook CS Mission, Daybrook Bridge Buildings, Mansfield Road.

Northumberland

Blyth – Chapel House Sanctuary, 9 Arthur Street.

Oxfordshire

Abingdon – CS Church, Fitzharry's Common Room, Wooton Road.
Oxford – (GW and SNU) CS Church, 34 Oxford Road, Cowley.
Oxford – CS Church, 11a Middle Way, Summertown, Oxford.

Salop

Shrewsbury – Saint Lukes CS Church, Morris Hall, Bilstone.

Shrewsbury – CS Temple of Light, Meeting Hall, Mount Pleasant Road.

Somerset

Bridgwater – CS Church, Queen Street.

Yeovil – Nazarene CS Church, 165 Westcoker Road.

Staffordshire

Burton-on-Trent – Horninglow CS Church, Farm Road, Horninglow.

Hednesford – Progressive CS Church, 23 Market Street.

Newcastle-under-Lyme – Light of Christ GWCS Church, Senior Citizens' Centre, Hanover Street.

Suffolk

Ipswich – CS Church and Healing Sanctuary, 'The Beeches', 131 Woodbridge Road.

Ipswich – CS Church, 'The Cedars', 46 Anglesea Road.

Lowestoft – Spastic Centre, Till Road.

Surrey

Farnham – CS Church, WVS Buildings, Gostrey Club, East Street.

North Cheam – Red Cross Hall, Malden Road.

Wallington and Carshalton – Hackbridge Hall, London Road.

Walton-on-Thames – CS Church, Halfway.

Woking – Sanctuary of Light, Room 4, Centre Halls.

East Sussex

Bexhill-on-Sea – CS Church, 24 Station Road.
Eastbourne – CS Church, 1b Cavendish Avenue.
Hastings – CS Church, 2/3 Claremont (end of Robertson Street).

West Sussex

Burgess Hill – Edith May Healing Sanctuary, 132 Chanctonbury Road.
Chichester – CS Church, 38 Southgate.
Worthing – CS Church, 6 Broadwater Road.

Tyne and Wear

Newcastle-upon-Tyne – Higher Thought CS Church, 247a Westgate Road.
South Shields – CS Church and Healing Centre, 42 Chichester Road.

North Yorkshire

York – CS Church, 41 Micklegate.

West Yorkshire

Kirkby (South) – Psychic and Healing Centre, 54 White Apron Street, near Pontefract.
Leeds – GW Sanctuary, 14 Clarendon Road.
Pudsey – Nisus CSC, 42 Town Street, Farsley, Pudsey.

Channel Islands

Jersey – GWCS Church, Dorset Street, Saint Helier.

Isle of Man

Douglas – GWCS Church, Duke's Street.

Scotland Central

Grangemouth – CS Mission, 'Janville', La Porte Precinct.
Falkirk – CS Church, Burnhead Lane, Falkirk.

Grampian

Lossiemouth – CSC Burgh Court Room, High Street.

Strathclyde

Airdrie – Airdrie and Dist S Church, Community Centre,
  Graham Street.
Glasgow – GWCS Church, 14 West Princes Street.
Glasgow – CS Mission, City Hall, Albion Street.
Rothesay – New Rothesay S Group, East Princes Street.

Tayside

Dundee – Silver Star CS Church, 119 Nethergate.

Wales Clwyd

Rhyl – Sanctuary, 20 Bodfor Street.

West Glamorgan

Neath – Circle of Light CS Church, 42 The Parade.

South Glamorgan

Cadoxton – CS Church, Kenilworth Road.
Cardiff – Northcote CS Church, 1a Northcote Street,
Roath.

Gwent

Monmouth – CS Church, Red Cross Centre, Church
Street.

Gwynedd

Bangor – CS Church, 267 High Street.

Australia

Nowra – CS Church, Berry Street, Nowra, NSW (Secretary, Mrs E Austin, 16 Grant Avenue, Nowra 2540).

Austria

Vienna – Wien XVII, Palffygasse 14/4.

Canada

North Burnaby – CS Church, 7804, 17th Avenue, Burnaby, BC, Canada V3N 1MZ.

New Zealand

Auckland – Church of the Golden Light, 25 New North Road.
Christchurch – The New Age CS Centre, 61 Grafton Street.
Wanganui – Frontiersman Hall, 61 Dublin Street.

Republic of South Africa

Benoni – Church, 56 Lake Avenue, Benoni 1500.
Cape Town – Temple of Spiritual Fellowship, 310 Hycastle House, 58 Loop Street.
Johannesburg – 5 Princes Street, Troyville, P.O. Box 10147.
Port Elizabeth – PO Box 12201, Centra Hil 6006.

U.S.A.

Philadelphia – GWCS Church, 151 E Roosevelt Boulevard.
San Francisco – Metaphysical Centre, 420 Sutter Street.

Zimbabwe

Harare – CS Church, 2nd Street. Tel. Harare 36395 or 37244.

Free literature and specimen copies of *The Greater World* paper can be obtained on application, from The Greater World Association, 3 Lansdowne Road, Holland Park, London W11. (Tel: 01 727 7264)

7

Associations, Societies, Festivals, Bookshops and Journals

THE SPIRITUALIST ASSOCIATION OF GREAT BRITAIN
The World's Largest Spiritualist Association
(open 7 days a week)

Sunday services at 3 and 6pm
Forty mediums available for private and group appointments
Two demonstrations of clairvoyance and a lecture every weekday
Demonstrations on Saturdays and Sundays
Fully staffed restaurant and library

Amenities Available on Each Floor
Lower Ground Floor:
Restaurant, open seven days a week.
Ground Floor:
Reception Desk. The Book Shop (fully stocked with a comprehensive range of books on Spiritual, Spiritualistic and healing subjects). The Conan Doyle Hall, The Lord Dowding Wing and The Lounge, which is available to members and visitors.
First Floor:
The Oliver Lodge Hall and The Library.
Second Floor:
The Chapel, open daily for prayer and meditation for members and visitors.
Third Floor:
The entire floor is devoted to Spiritual healing, which is

available to members and non-members. Healing is given privately and without charge. A receptionist is on hand to help you with your healing appointments. Free-will donations are acceptable.

Fourth Floor:
Rooms 20–25 are used for private and group appointments and also for development classes.
An elevator serves all floors except the fourth floor, which can be reached via the stairway on the third floor.

We are fully aware that some people have had problems trying to contact us by telephone. So what is the problem? Times have changed. In earlier days when transport was cheap, members and visitors came into the Association to make their appointments. Now, because of high fares, they find it more economical and convenient to telephone us. The result is that we are now receiving three or four times the number of calls we accepted in earlier times. Why not try to write to us instead? If you know in advance when you want an appointment – do it by letter, remembering to enclose a stamped addressed envelope for an early reply. PLEASE BEAR IT IN MIND, WE ARE NOT IGNORING YOU, JUST DOING THE VERY BEST WE CAN.

Thank you,
The Secretary.

We are at: 33 Belgrave Square, London, SW1. Telephone: (01) 235 3351.
The office is open Monday to Friday 10am to 7.15pm. Saturday 10am to 5pm. Sunday 3pm to 8.15pm.
How to find us: Bus Routes: 2, 2b, 11, 16, 22, 25, 30, 36, 36b, 38, 52, 73, 74, 137 and 500.
Green Line: 704, 705, 707, 708, 714, 717, 718 and 719.
Piccadilly Line: Hyde Park Corner. Inner Circle: Victoria or Sloane Square.

COLLEGE OF PSYCHIC STUDIES

16 Queensbury Place, London SW7. Tel: (01) 589 3292

THE SOCIETY FOR PSYCHICAL RESEARCH

1 Adam and Eve Mews, London W8. Tel: (01) 937 8984

MIND – BODY – SPIRIT
THE SHOW FOR HEALTHY LIVING

Natural Living – Health & Healing – Yoga & Keep Fit – Psychic Phenomena – Organic Gardening – Mystical Arts & Crafts – UFOs – Astrology – Ancient Philosophies – Alternative Technology.

The London Festival for Mind Body Spirit is the largest and one of the most successful events of its kind in the world. Established in 1977, the great care with which it is prepared makes it a unique and stimulating occasion of truly international stature. It is a time for people to get absorbed in a fantastic variety of new interests and to have fun doing so.

Mind-Body-Spirit Festival, Olympia, London. Held annually in July.
Mind-Body-Spirit Festival, Los Angeles and San Francisco. Held annually in February and March respectively.
Psychics and Mystics Fayre. Held three times yearly in Birmingham, Bristol and London.
Further details on all the above events can be obtained from:
159 George Street, London W1. Tel: (01) 723 7256
Information on the USA Festivals can also be obtained from:
Unity-In-Diversity Council, World Trade Center, 350 S

Figueroa St, Los Angeles, California 90071. Tel: (213) 626 2062

Free advance booking programme from: 159 George Street, London W1.

Psychic Book Society & SAGB Book Club

Your chance to collect your own personal library of first-class psychic books at well below publishers' prices.

For many years the Psychic Book Society has offered its members the latest Psychic Press books at 25 per cent discount as they are published. Now we will also offer well-produced volumes on similar themes from other publishing houses. The discount you get will be at least 25 per cent; in some cases it will be almost 50 per cent.

All titles will be carefully chosen to give you a broad range of psychic topics at reasonable cost. They will be identical in every way to copies available in the shops, except that you will get them more cheaply.

Psychic Press will continue to publish books and they will likewise be available to PBS members at a considerable saving.

It costs you nothing to join the Psychic Book Society. You need only sign a form agreeing to accept each book which will automatically be sent to you, along with an invoice showing the normal publishers' price and the discount price you pay.

Approximately six titles will be selected for members each year. They will be either paperbacks or reasonably-priced hardbound books.

Address all enquiries to: Psychic Book Society, Psychic Press Ltd, Freepost, London WC2.

Psychic News Bookshop

Callers and browsers welcomed. Buy from Britain's largest selection of psychic books. Send for book list. Closed on Saturdays.

20 Earlham Street, London WC2. Tel: (01) 240 3032/3/4

Robinson & Watkins
Comprehensive selection of books. Centrally located off the Charing Cross Road.
21 Cecil Court, London WC2. Tel: (01) 836 2182

The Spiritualist Association of Great Britain
Book Shop
Fully stocked with a comprehensive range of books on Spiritual, Spiritualistic and healing subjects.
Ground Floor, 33 Belgrave Square, London SW1. Tel: (01) 235 3351

Theosophical Bookshop
68 Great Russell Street, London WC1. Tel: (01) 405 2309

Mysteries
Psychic supplies – crystals, cards, pendulums etc, and a variety of books.
9 Monmouth Street, London WC2. Tel: (01) 240 3688

Horoscope
Monthly astrology magazine.

Light
Quarterly journal of the College of Psychic Studies,
16 Queensbury Place, London SW7.

Prediction
Incorporating Weekly Horoscope and Fantasy
A popular style magazine covering astrology and all aspects of the occult. Articles include astrological forecasts for the month, the Tarot, palmistry, graphology, dream meanings, occult question time and book reviews.

Psychic News and its sister monthly magazine
Two Worlds

Psychic News is Britain's only independent Spiritualist weekly with a weekly readership of 100,000. Founded in 1932 by Maurice Barbanell, *Psychic News* can be obtained from your newsagent or it can be sent by post to your home anywhere in the world. Subscription enquiries should be addressed to: Psychic Press Ltd., Freepost, London WC2. Subscription enquiries for *Two Worlds* should be mailed to the same address.

The Spiritualist Gazette

A monthly journal with news and reports about Spiritualist activity and psychic-related subjects. Published by the Spiritualist Association of Great Britain, 33 Belgrave Square, London SW1. Tel: (01) 235 3351

8

One for the Road

The North American Indian has always held a place of importance for those mediums who acknowledge their reliance on Indian spirit guides. Many people, knowing little about the Indian philosophy of the comparatively recent past, tend to misinterpret the true reason for an emphasis on what might seem to them to be a rather quaint and alien culture.

The following extract, taken from a non-psychic publication, should highlight those traditional Indian spiritual values which are held in high esteem by many Western mediums, apart from which it is a fascinating statement about a people who lived by a well-defined spiritual philosophy.

This extract is quoted from: *Minority Groups Report No. 31: The Original Americans: US Indians* by James Wilson.

Underpinning the Indians' social structures, and pervading every aspect of their lives, were the tribal religions which – despite enormous local variations in form and ritual – were in many of their fundamentals extraordinarily similar. It would be difficult to over-stress the importance of religion to the native American. Most Indians believed in a cosmic unity which embraced man, animals, plants, elements and immensely influential but generally invisible spiritual forces. Human society had to co-operate and live harmoniously with the other components in this universal whole, and this entailed not only the performance of prescribed rituals and the use of shamans or priests to mediate between man and spirit, but also adherence to certain strict rules and disciplines in the conduct of hunting, eating and other everyday activities.

The majority of Indians believed that 'in the beginning' a deity or culture hero had given 'the people' – as many of the tribes called themselves in their own languages – the land they inhabited and instructions concerning how they could live there efficiently and in accord with the overall scheme of things. This information, embodying the Indians' immense knowledge of the nature and resources of their own areas, was expressed in myths and stories and handed on from one generation to the next; it generally emphasized the importance of virtues such as responsibility, courage, compliance and respect for life as well as teaching the skills required for the provision of food and other necessaries and laying down the way in which they were to be practised. The individual Indian was judged by how nearly he lived up to the divinely-ordained ideal, and celebrations were held annually or more frequently which, in a mystic way, relived the original drama of 'the people' and heightened the Indians' awareness of their sacred obligations to the givers and sustainers of life.

The contrast between the Indians' religious perceptions and those of the European has caused enormous misunderstandings and conflicts over the last five centuries. The problem carries far beyond the obvious clashes between evangelizing Christians and adherents to traditional native beliefs. The Indians' deep-seated sense that their land and their way of life are gifts with which the Creator has solemnly entrusted them has embarrassed and bewildered whites, who find it difficult to comprehend why many native people have fought so long and so stubbornly, whether through active or passive resistance, to cling to their old ways and their homelands when they are hopelessly outnumbered and have been offered all the – apparently greater – benefits of an alternative civilization. The pragmatic European mentality, which sees in technology a means to adapt any environment to the needs of a particular human culture, tends to dismiss as fanciful and childishly superstitious the Indian's reverence for his land, which has led him to take the opposite approach and adapt his culture to the nature and potential of a particular environment. Indians, for their part, have frequently failed to understand the European concept of land as property which can be disposed of as the owner wishes – and when they *have* understood it the idea has generally appalled them. The special relationship between a people, the land on which they have lived since 'the beginning' and the food it produces to sustain them is, to the traditional Indian, something personal, mystical and profound that can only be abandoned by an act that is tantamount to the betrayal of a deeply-loved parent. The notion that the earth was his mother was not understood symbolically, but taken literally by the aboriginal American; even today the traditional people of Taos Pueblo refuse to plough their reservation because it would be tantamount to tearing their mother's flesh.

The complete *Report No. 31, The Original Americans: US Indians* (1980 Edition), is currently priced at £1.20. The Minority Rights Group enjoy consultative status with the United Nations (ECOSOC). Their address is: Minority Rights Group, Benjamin Franklin House, 36 Craven Street, London WC2.

INNOCENT VOICES IN MY EAR

Doris Stokes

with Linda Dearsley

Doris Stokes' first book, VOICES IN MY EAR, was a bestseller. So was the sequel, MORE VOICES IN MY EAR.

Now in INNOCENT VOICES IN MY EAR, she tells of her special relationship with children and her psychic communications with children of every age; from the heroic young men of the Falklands War, to the 16-year-old hostage of a ruthless gunman and the tragic stars who died too young: John Lennon, Marc Bolan and Richard Beckinsale.

Doris Stokes has astonished the world with her extraordinary powers and here in her typical down-to-earth way she explains how she copes with everything from haunted restaurants to murder-mysteries. But most of all she talks about the children, all of those innocent children who belong to her spirit family on the other side.

Futura Publications
Non-Fiction/Autobiography
0 7088 2320 3

MORE VOICES IN MY EAR

Doris Stokes

with Linda Dearsley

Since the publication of her astonishing life story, the bestselling VOICES IN MY EAR, medium Doris Stokes has been besieged by requests from her many new friends to recount more of her unique experiences.

Now in MORE VOICES IN MY EAR she tells of how her extraordinary psychic powers have helped the family of one of the Yorkshire Ripper victims, enabled the late actor Peter Finch to communicate with his wife, and brought hope to the parents of young children who have disappeared in strange circumstances all over the world.

Writing of her experiences in Australia and New Zealand, America and Canada and in Ireland, Doris now gives a complete picture of life in the spirit world and never fails to comfort and encourage all her many friends and followers.

Futura Publications
Non-Fiction/Autobiography
0 7088 2100 6

VOICES IN MY EAR
THE AUTOBIOGRAPHY OF A MEDIUM

Doris Stokes
with Linda Dearsley

SHE'S HELPED TO SOLVE MURDER CASES.

SHE FILLED THE SYDNEY OPERA HOUSE THREE NIGHTS IN A ROW.

ONCE, SHE EVEN HAD TO CONVINCE A MAN HE WAS DEAD.

NOW SHE'S WRITTEN HER OWN ASTONISHING LIFE STORY.

Her name is Doris Stokes.

As a child she often saw things others couldn't. During the War she was officially informed her husband had been killed. At the height of her grief she was visited by her long-dead father and told her husband was alive and would return.

But joy turned to grief when her father reappeared to warn of the impending death of her healthy baby son.

Both predictions came true.

And Doris Stokes had to accept the fact that she possessed an amazing gift. Exceptional psychic powers that over the years of her extraordinary life have brought joy and comfort to thousands of people.

Futura Publications
Non-Fiction/Autobiography
0 7088 1786 6

All Futura Books are available at your bookshop or newsagent, or can be ordered from the following address:
Futura Books, Cash Sales Department,
P.O. Box 11, Falmouth, Cornwall.

Please send cheque or postal order (no currency), and allow 45p for postage and packing for the first book plus 20p for the second book and 14p for each additional book ordered up to a maximum charge of £1.63 in U.K.

Customers in Eire and B.F.P.O. please allow 45p for the first book, 20p for the second book plus 14p per copy for the next 7 books, thereafter 8p per book.

Overseas customers please allow 75p for postage and packing for the first book and 21p per copy for each additional book.